D1784796

Neoplatonist Stew

Or,

How Sacramentalism, Mysticism, and Theurgy Corrupted Christian Theology

Neoplatonist Stew

Or,

How Sacramentalism, Mysticism, and Theurgy Corrupted Christian Theology

by

Paul A. Hughes

Library of Congress Cataloguing in Publication Data
Hughes, Paul A., 1957–
Includes footnotes and index.
ISBN 978-1-304-54918-1

ON THE COVERS: Front inset: "The School of Athens by Raphael," public domain, as established under U. S. law in Bridgeman v. Corel, 36 F. Supp. 2d 191 (S.D.N.Y. 1999), supported by the U. S. Supreme Court in Feist v. Rural, 499 U.S. 340 (1991)[1], applying the First Amendment to the Constitution and the Copyright Act of 1976. Copyright claims to public domain works risk the criminal provisions of Section 506 of the Copyright Act for fraudulent use of a copyright notice. Back inset: "Invasion of the Body Snatchers" movie poster parody, created by the author, including public domain clip art, protected by the First Amendment as established by Hustler Magazine, Inc., v. Falwell, 485 U.S., *et al.*, protection for parody speech. Background images, both covers: Created and fully owned by the author.

Contents

To all those who believe the Word of God,

seek His face,

and obey His Spirit.

ἀλλὰ τοῦτό ἐστιν τὸ εἰρημένον διὰ τοῦ προφήτου Ἰωήλ,

Καὶ ἔσται ἐν ταῖς ἐσχάταις ἡμέραις, λέγει ὁ θεός, ἐκχεῶ ἀπὸ τοῦ πνεύματός μου ἐπὶ πᾶσαν σάρκα, καὶ προφητεύσουσιν οἱ υἱοὶ ὑμῶν καὶ αἱ θυγατέρες ὑμῶν, καὶ οἱ νεανίσκοι ὑμῶν ὁράσεις ὄψονται, καὶ οἱ πρεσβύτεροι ὑμῶν ἐνυπνίοις ἐνυπνιασθήσονται·

καί γε ἐπὶ τοὺς δούλους μου καὶ ἐπὶ τὰς δούλας μου ἐν ταῖς ἡμέραις ἐκείναις ἐκχεῶ ἀπὸ τοῦ πνεύματός μου, καὶ προφητεύσουσιν.

~Acts 2:16-18

Other Works by the Author

Christ in Us: The Exalted Christ and the Indwelling of the Holy Spirit (Liberty, TX: God's Trombone, 2006).

Christ within You! The Indwelling of the Holy Spirit, 2nd ed. (Liberty, TX: God's Trombone, 1993; rpt. ed., 2008).

William Sherlock, *A Practical Discourse concerning Death*, edited, annotated, and with historical introduction by Paul A. Hughes (Liberty, TX: God's Trombone, 2007).

Divine Parodies & Holy Histories: With Select Poems: Illustrations of Gospel Truth (Liberty, TX: God's Trombone, 2007).

"How Did Man Change When Adam Fell?" *Paraclete* 23 (Fall 1989):20-23.

"Speaking God's Message: The Holy Spirit and the Human Mind," *Paraclete* 26 (Spring 1992):17-22.

"Worship in the Second Century: The Spiritual Dimension," *Paraclete* 21 (Fall 1987):20-25.

Subscribe to the Author's Web Sites:

Bible Q&A	*http://biblequstion.wordpress.com*
Casting Out Devils	*http://ekballo.wordpress.com*
Paul Hughes Ministry	*http://www.facebook.com/pages/Paul-Hughes-Bible-Ministry-Music/191666-770853802?ref=hl*

Download the companion chart for this book at http://biblequestion.wordpress.com/2013/09/26/-pagan-origins-of-sacramentalism-part-6/.

Preface

The impetus for undertaking this study was a series of events and discussions, due to which I became increasingly aware of Biblically unsound, non-Pentecostal doctrines and practices being promoted by some of my own, ostensibly Pentecostal peers. These items of concern include certain worship leaders wishing to restore liturgy to worship, a number of ministers favoring an approach to the Lord's Supper in terms of sacramental efficacy—both on premises such as reconnecting to ancient, historical Christianity and restoring a purportedly fuller, richer form of worship full of "mystery"—and the pursuit of mystical transcendence or "union" with Christ. At least one minister proposed that sacraments be used evangelistically, as if an unbeliever might undergo some kind of existential realization through the act of partaking. The "capper" was the occasion of my own fellowship's national leaders inviting a Contemplative Prayer teacher/guru to speak at its annual meeting (2013).

My immediate purpose in this research project was to marshal evidence to prove to the proponents of these doctrines and practices, first, that they are contrary to Scripture and, moreover, that they are of specious nature and origin, namely, Pagan and counter to Biblical, Pentecostal spirituality.

As more astute readers will realize from the manner in which the series unfolds, it was a process of discovery. I literally did not know where the trail would lead as I began to publish the initial parts of the series online. I asked the questions first, reviewed the overall problem, then looked for answers. I saw that Ernst Käsemann posited the origins of Sacramentalism in Gnostic religion, while the trend among recent scholarship seems to be to discount significant Gnostic influence, as well as that of the Mystery Religions. The fact that those influences were part of the mix is undeniable, but to what extent were they to blame? For the most part, those strains seem to have "petered out" over time as the religions themselves faded. I looked toward Far Eastern influences, but found little and only late evidence, as well as the suggestion that the early influence flowed the opposite direction, from Greek philosophy eastward.

The more I searched and read, the more I began to discover references to Neoplatonism and terms that I had never heard before, such as

Theurgy, hieratic, and *apophatic.* At one point I experienced a *eureka* moment as I began to realize that I had discovered a major component of external influence on Christian theology, which by its dimensions and repeated injection over many centuries promises to represent the main stream.

In order to begin to comprehend the complex relationships of the various historic theologians and how they passed along these external doctrines, I assembled a diagram, after the manner of a flow chart or organizational chart. At the core of the chart is the basic skeletal structure that I was able to determine first by following Robert Grant's history of Bible interpretation,[1] further fleshed out with the help of Father Andrew Louth's very helpful walk through Neoplatonic history, to which I added as I went along from many additional sources. I included only connections to Neoplatonic influences which I found explicitly documented in the sources, ignoring mere suspicions and implications. Unconnected personages were in some cases included on an incidental basis, only in order to demonstrate their relativity. The latest version of the chart may be downloaded from my blog using the link printed on introductory page vi.

My biggest surprise was that the influx of Neoplatonism and Theurgy has long been an "open secret" among Catholic theologians and many Protestants, though not one often disclosed on a popular, lay level, for some obvious, partisan, and none too spiritual reasons. That Thomas Aquinas, for example, adopted many theological ideas from the Theurgist known as Pseudo-Dionysius is "not to be spoken of"; or rather, to be explained away. The usual approaches are to insist that historical theologians simply utilized Platonic and Neoplatonic terminology and categories in order to systematize and refine Christian theology; or, less scientifically, to claim that Neoplatonism and Theurgy have been somehow "baptized" or sanctified by the good intentions of their Christian advocates and by the beneficial use to which they have now been applied. It is an old ploy, in the light of much Scripture to the contrary, to submit that God would not allow well-intentioned believers to fall into error. In retrospect, I have to regard either approach as ranging from disingenuousness to an exercise in self-delusion to outright deception.

---

[1] Robert M. Grant with David Tracy, *A Short History of the Interpretation of the Bible,* 2nd ed. (Phila: Fortress Press, 1984).

Regretfully, the initial response from those proponents of Sacramentalism and Mysticism for whom I intended this report has been to dismiss it out-of-hand, without due, objective consideration, often with hostility, variously accusing me of making unfounded assertions, lacking the ability to comprehend and "work with" my sources, misrepresenting the facts, having malicious intent, etc., yet never bothering, to date, to adduce a single scrap of disproof, and in many cases, I feel assured, never having done more than skim its text. The chart, which in itself goes a long way toward establishing my thesis of influence and connectedness throughout church history, has been said to have a lot of nice colors but otherwise to be of little value and based on ignorance. Critics point out theologians I did not include, and connections I did not make, as if thereby proving the chart to be "a glass half empty." It therefore appears, from these and other evidences, that those who have bought into these belief systems, or modes of understanding Christianity, are heavily invested in them and committed to protecting them from criticism, as well as promoting their advancement, at the expense of objectivity and brotherhood.

Finally, proponents raise the question whether Pentecostal spirituality itself is not mystical, as if the New Testament model would then validate any and all forms of Christianized Mysticism, a supposition highly flawed in that it is baldly *non sequitur*. Even in Scripture, there are false prophets, miracles, and spiritualities which could likewise be classified as mystical, but in no way created equal. Mysticism is by nature ethereal and consequently difficult to study as well as define. In this study, we are targeting our observation at that which is contrary to Scripture, specifically the Neoplatonic as well as Theurgical. Neoplatonism entails an *ascent* to God *via* contemplation and self-realization, toward metaphysical attainments and ultimately self-divination. New Testament Spirit Baptism, in contrast, is a *descent* of God himself, by measure and by grace, into mortal flesh, devoid of its own attainments, but being granted *immediate* access to God; immediate, *imputed* attainment, *i.e.*, eschatological righteousness and Eternal Life; and immediate empowerment for service, overcoming sin, and witnessing the Gospel. Those persons so exercised by the indwelling Spirit are instruments for divine use, not in themselves divinized except in terms of faithfulness and exemplary behavior; divinization is only to be realized when one is ultimately "changed" (1 Cor 15:51 f.) in a bodily, apocalyptic Resurrection. Moreover, whereas Neoplatonism is a psychological phenomenon of mental and physical discipline with the intent of altered consciousness, New Testament spirituality is a spiritual phenomenon of divine action in fulfillment of God's prophetic Promise.

I therefore leave it to the astute, objective reader to be the judge of both the source material and the conclusions drawn therefrom, in the light of Scripture, history, and objectivity, and the outcome to the Lord.

Rev. Paul A. Hughes
Liberty, Texas
October, 2013

Chapter 1. The Problem Stated

There is currently a movement afoot within Pentecostal ranks to accommodate Sacramental Realism/spiritual efficacy/"means of grace" in our doctrine. Its proponents hold that the Spirit moves and is conveyed in various ways through the action of taking Communion. However, such doctrine represents an alternate spirituality and route of spiritual efficacy, not taught in the New Testament, in competition with Holy Spirit Baptism as actually taught by Christ and the Apostles.

Pentecostalism stands in contrast and inherent opposition to regarding the Lord's Supper and Water Baptism as anything more than symbolic remembrances, testimonies, and ordinances. To say more suggests "means of grace" or spiritual efficacy that is contrary to clear Scripture describing the abiding means of grace, guidance, and empowerment through Holy Spirit Baptism. If the Spirit moves through sacraments (a view unsupportable from Scripture), then Spirit Baptism would be rendered superfluous, as would the *charismata*. Stretching "this is my body" beyond metaphor to "Sacramental Realism" is externally derived and exegetically unwarranted.

The *Paraclete* statements in John 14-16 contain not the merest suggestion relating to sacraments, nor do the commands to "tarry" for "the Promise of the Father" (Spirit Baptism), nor is there any positive command in the New Testament to take sacraments in order that the Spirit may come.

What Is Sacramental Realism?

The basic idea of Sacramental Realism is that the bread of the Lord's supper is actually, spiritually, Christ's body, and the drink is actually, spiritually, Christ's blood. Extreme views include *Transubstantiation* which Catholics believe, and *Consubstantiation* which various mainline Protestants believe. Those traditions also tend toward *Sacerdotalism*, the idea that salvific efficacy and "grace" are conveyed by a priest in dispensing sacraments. Thus Holy Communion to some is made the "means of grace" in order to receive or maintain salvation, which would make excommunication a matter of losing one's soul.

Pentecostals who advocate Sacramentalism of course tend to distance themselves from those extremes, if only to avoid criticism, and speak in terms of spiritual feelings or some kind of *existential* realization that taking the Lord's Supper evokes to them. They also suggest that healings and other *charismata* may occur through taking sacraments, or a realization of *Mystical Union* with Christ. The late Howard M. Ervin was a well-known Pentecostal supportive of Sacramental Realism.

The traditional Pentecostal view, and the exegetically-derived view, is that the Lord's Supper is a remembrance/memorial observance, and the bread and drink metaphorical/symbolic of Christ's actual body and blood, such that our participation is a confession and public testimony of our reliance on the *actual* sacrifice of Christ which they represent.

Let me be clear: in no way do I dispute that the Holy Spirit can move upon Spirit-filled people during the Lord's Supper—in fact, I would be disappointed if He did not—and *charismata* also be manifested. But I vehemently dispute the suggestion that the act of taking sacraments was intended by Christ as a "means of grace," in itself, either for salvation, or the Baptism in the Holy Spirit, or the *manifestations* of the Spirit, alternative to the promised, conventional, normative, expected, and didactic picture and source of Spirit Baptism and spiritual activity found in the New Testament. Note that Spirit Baptism is never directly associated with participation in the Lord's Supper anywhere in Scripture.

An Argument from Silence

When reading *The Body* by John A. T. Robinson, one notes that he recites considerable exegesis regarding the Body of Christ, but when he finally introduces *Sacramentalism*, he takes a great leap past exegesis, and can provide no exegetical basis for that doctrine. Similarly, Howard M. Ervin (*Conversion-Initiation and the Baptism in the Holy Spirit*) offers but scant exegetical proof; rather resorts to a logico-philosophical argument fraught with jargon. Others resort to church history and historical theology. The fact is, the Sacramental view cannot be supported exegetically from Scripture, *because it is not there*!

Can Christians be fully obedient if we do not believe that the person and work of the Holy Spirit, which is "the Promise of the Father" (Acts 1:4, 2:33), is *central* to the Plan of Redemption? Why did Christ "have to go away" (Jn 14:28, 16:7) in order to send the Holy Spirit? Why did Jesus tell the Apostles to "tarry in Jerusalem" till they be "filled"? Why did the Holy Spirit fill all those at Pentecost, at Ephesus, at Joppa, and Peter, Paul, Philip and his daughters, Agabus—if they could just seek "Real Presence" or "Mystical Union" instead? Why were potential converts promised "the gift of the Holy Spirit," and not "the gift of *Real Presence/Mystical Union*" (see Acts 2:38, 8:15 ff., 9:17, 11:16, 19:2 ff.)?

(We must not be like the "Oneness" schismatics who in 1915 admitted that one cannot find the "Jesus only" message in the Bible, one has to get it by revelation. Revelation, on the contrary, is subject to exegetical judgment in accordance with the plain teaching of Scripture, and ought not simply be accepted at face value. That which is exegetically unsupportable is at best specious.)

To garner "Real Presence" or "sacrament" from the few scant passages on the Lord's Supper is, for starters, an "argument from silence"; and further, a preconceived and external theology. It is not allowing the figurative language (symbol, metaphor) to act as intended, but forces the text into extreme, out-of-context literalism. It is no more literal in the passages in question, than when Jesus said, "I am the Bread of life" (John 6—contrasting himself from physical bread, while teaching no one to partake of such), "I am the Door," "I am the Road," or allusions to "living water." Note that He did not then go on to teach his Disciples to venerate or celebrate bread, doors, roads, or water.

The Lord's Supper is, in two New Testament witnesses, a "remembrance" or "memorial." In three witnesses, it is a "testament," in terms of a testimony of God's promise. There is no hint of literal Spirit-grace accompanying the elements in any way whatsoever.

Pagan Influences

Ernst Käsemann (*Essays on New Testament Themes*) argues for "*Real Presence*," but spends all of one page and scant exegesis on it. For his "proof" he relies largely on his construct of Paul's version of the Lord's Supper, which treats Paul's concept as "adopted and adapted" from the *Gnostic* myths of the Archetypal Man or Redeemer.

Indeed, to Käsemann, all of Paul's christology is drawn from Gnosticism.[1]

As such, Käsemann describes the taking of the sacrament as conveying the *Pneuma* (the "New Lord" to replace the lords of this world), which "is an epiphany of the exalted Lord, who becomes manifest in it.... Therefore the sacrament effects the transformation of man."[2] "And we become members of his Body because the Christ enters into us as *Pneuma*."[3] "The eucharistic cup mediates participation in this divine order because it mediates participation in the death of Jesus on which this order is based."[4]

According to Gnostic ideology, "Man is the object of this struggle between the powers. ... he finds redemption when the *Pneuma* invades his earthly nature and recaptures him for the heavenly world. The state of being resulting from this event is called 'metamorphosis'. While it only comes to final fruition in death, which is liberation from earthly matter, it nevertheless has a proleptic fulfilment in the cultic act."[5] "Because man can undergo a change of lordship, the possibility of an existential transformation exists. And this is precisely what does happen in the sacramental event, when we are endowed with the gift of the Pneuma."[6]

Colin Brown's *New International Dictionary of New Testament Theology* (*NIDNTT*) likewise sees contemporary pagan origins for the concept of "Real Presence," (though not at all for Paul's own christology, of course—that is Käsemann's pet theory).

> In the ancient religions eating and drinking were mostly formal meals, i.e. acts of public or private fellowship linked with the sacred.... Families, clans and religious fellowships received a share in divine power through the common meal, which represented their union with the deity. The origin of the sacred character of the meal is connected with magic concepts, according

---

[1] Ernst Käsemann, *Essays on New Testament Themes* (Phila.: Fortress Press, 1982), p. 109.
[2] *Ibid.*, p. 118.
[3] *Ibid.*, p. 115.
[4] *Ibid.*, p. 128.
[5] *Ibid.*, p. 116.
[6] *Ibid.*, p. 117. See my article on the Gnostic View of Christ as Redeemer or Archetypal Man: http://biblequestion.wordpress.com/2010/04/16/the-gnostic-christ/.

to which the divine is embodied in material things (animism...)....
In short, there was nothing which unites man and man, and man
and God, more than eating and drinking....[1]

The Damage Being Done

One finds no ready source of statistics on how many Pentecostal or
their leaders endorse or practice *Sacramental Realism*, *Mystical Union*,
Contemplative Prayer, or other alternate spiritualities. In many cases,
it is a matter of degree rather than mere influence. For example, Pentecostal worship is in a very broad sense "mystical" (as Mystics themselves note) but teaching that one can achieve spiritual grace through
taking sacraments, or Mystical Union with Christ through Contemplative Prayer, fasting, etc., is contradictory to a Pentecostal theology, and
extreme.

In my experience, people who believe in Mystical Union and Sacramental Realism soon begin to distance themselves from Scripture, the
need for scriptural authority, and in fact begin to see themselves as
"above" Scripture, purportedly having achieved some kind of higher
personal association with Christ. I am finding that more and more
erstwhile Pentecostals, novice Pentecostals, and pseudo-Pentecostals
are accepting these and other alternate spiritualities, abandoning or
misunderstanding Pentecostalism, both historic and New Testament-
based, apparently not discerning the differences.

Pentecostalism is the very doctrine of Christ and the Apostles,
clearly taught and exemplified in Scripture, being the empowerment
that Christ intended and promised for his Church through his Holy
Spirit till Christ returns in glory. This "grace," as Paul discovered, "is
sufficient."

---

[1] B. Klappert, "Lord's Supper" in *The New International Dictionary of New Testament Theology*, vol. 2, Colin Brown, gen. ed. (Grand Rapids: Zondervan), p. 520.

Chapter 2. The Great Exegetical Leap

Many attempts to prove and defend *Sacramental Realism* from Scripture have been made over the centuries, by exegesis and analogy, which the honest inquirer is free to consult. The fact that such defenses are numerous and readily available speaks manifestly of the suspect nature of the doctrine, from the lengths deemed necessary to bolster it. Let us dispense with exegetical *minutiae* and proceed to core concepts and questions, which will suffice. So what are the Sacramentalists' proofs from Scripture, and how do they stack up?

> What are the actual phenomena in the New Testament in relation to the sacraments, especially as they reflect on the issue of sacramentalism or sacramental realism? First of all it is quite conspicuous that the New Testament has very little to say concerning the sacraments. The word "sacrament" in a technical sense does not even appear in the New Testament. And there is nothing at all concerning sacramental efficacy as such.[1]

At the Last Supper, Jesus said, "This is my body," and "This is my blood." Under normal circumstances, the metaphorical nature of these statements would be a "given," and only excepted in the case of "special" circumstances, such as a special mode of interpretation to suit special circumstances, or a claim of "special revelation" as to what Jesus "really meant." Hence Sacramentalists insist that when Jesus said, "This is my body," He meant his actual body, and in the case of the wine, his actual blood, if only in a spiritual but certainly in a nuanced, qualified, literalized sense.

But no, there is no inherent reason to regard these metaphors any more literally than Jesus' "I am" statements such as "I am the Bread of Life," "I am the Door," and "I am the Path." Certainly, each of these metaphors points to a literal object, comparing one thing to another and describing a similarity; but that is a far cry from over-identifying, "this is literally that."

---

[1] Daniel A. Tappeiner, "Hermeneutics, the Analogy of Faith and New Testament Sacramental Realism," *Evangelical Quarterly* 49 (1977):44 f.

A Tie Unraveling

Sacramentalists point to alleged parallels in the miracle of turning water into wine at Cana, and references to his body as "bread" in John's Gospel, Chapter 6. They say, for instance, that the turning of water into wine proves a spiritual reality (a notably vague concept) in the substance itself, as acted upon by Jesus. However, in both the Cana episode and that on the Mount in John 6, the miracles were unpremeditated, and occasioned in answer to perceived needs. At Cana, Jesus was persuaded by his mother to rescue the Wedding Master from embarrassment; on the Mount, Jesus was concerned with the people going hungry. There is no reason to presume intent on Jesus' part to institute sacramental practices in these episodes.

Not only is Jesus' self-identification as "the Bread of Life" and "the True Bread" in John 6 not supportive of Sacramental Realism, but conclusively tells against it. In the episode, throngs who were following him in order to witness miracles pursued Jesus to a remote place, where He miraculously fed them by multiplying loaves and fishes. Afterward, the throngs followed him in order to get free bread. Jesus corrected them: they should labor to get eternal food, not perishable (6:27). They demanded that Jesus give them such eternal food, and a sign from God, suggesting that He call down manna to confirm his words. To them, manna was "bread from heaven," *i.e.*, "spiritual bread." No, indeed, said Jesus, "Your fathers ate manna in the wilderness, and are dead" (6:58). In short, no physical bread, even "from heaven," is truly spiritual or eternal, and neither God's presence, nor blessing, nor salvation are inherently associated with it.

Much less do we see divine presence attached to the wine at Cana. Note that there is, first, no wine present on the Mount, and no bread at Cana. At Cana, one sees no association of the wine with blood, nor to salvation or eternal life. Late in John 6, Jesus speaks of blood but not of wine. It takes no close examination to conclude that the parallels are scant, institutional content nil, and support for *Mystical Presence* absent.

Substance versus Spirit

In *The New International Dictionary of New Testament Theology* citation, "Lord's Supper" (vol. 2, p. 535), the "editor," (may we assume Colin Brown himself?) speaks of the purported Johannine version of the Last Supper found in John 6:

> It is commonly assumed that Jn. 6 is about the Lord's Supper, even though there is no hint in the text itself to any form of meal, liturgical or otherwise. ... Jn. 6 is not about the Lord's Supper; rather, the Lord's Supper is about what is described in Jn. 6. It concerns that eating and drinking which is belief in Christ (6:35), which is eternal life (6:54), and which in other words is described as abiding in him (6:56).... Jn. is, in effect, saying that the whole of the Christian life should be characterized by this kind of feeding on Christ and that this is what the sacramental meal of the church is really about.[1]

To continue in that vein, faith, spirituality, and worship of Christ has nothing at all to do with the substance of the bread and wine. The elements can be entirely absent. Worship of any kind, even if one "speak[s] with the tongues of men and angels," "bestow[s] all [his] goods to feed the poor," and "gives [his] body to be burned," is empty as "sounding brass, or a tinkling cymbal" (1 Cor 13:1-3) in itself; nor can "the blood of bulls and goats ... take away sins" (Heb 10:4). Likewise, simply partaking of the bread and wine, as such, without "discerning the Lord's body" (recognizing what the emblems stand for, symbolically, 1 Cor 11:29) and "examining oneself" (accounting whether one is "worthy" and is "in the faith," 11:27, 2 Cor 13:5) is worthless towards eternal life: rather, brings "judgment."

One wonders how sacramental concepts of ritual and substance toward salvation and worship could possibly be resolved with the "Spirit and Truth" worship Christ foretold to the Samaritan woman (John 4). Such worship is not to be found in temple worship, with a temporal priesthood and sacrifices, but in spiritual worship with a true heart toward God and interaction with the Holy Spirit, for "God is spirit." Those who worship "in Spirit and Truth" require neither substance nor sacrifice. Those who worship otherwise, risk worshipping "you know not what" (4:22).

---

[1] Klappert, p. 535.

Leapfrogging Exegesis

But for the most part, lacking unambiguous exegetical support, Sacramentalists take a "great leap" past exegesis to unwarranted assertions. In his popular study, *The Body*, John A. T. Robinson makes such a leap.[1] He first expends most of 46 pages in an exegetical synthesis designed to establish his concept of the Church as equivalent to the Body of Christ (which, as he describes, one enters through Baptismal Regeneration, see pp. 44, 46 f., 72, 75, 79-82). Abruptly, as if to draw a conclusion, he introduces the unfounded statement, "The Christian, because he is in the Church and united with Him in the sacraments, is part of Christ's body so literally that all that happened in and through that body in the flesh can be repeated in and through him now" (p. 47), which he afterward neglects to substantiate, exegetically. Proceeding, Robinson insists upon literalizing the Body, as well as the sacraments, to an extreme. Christians, he says, are "in literal fact the risen organism of Christ's person in all its concrete reality" (p. 51). Further, "to say that the Church is the body of Christ is no more of a metaphor than to say that the flesh of the incarnate Jesus or the bread of the Eucharist is the body of Christ" (*Ibid.*). "In so far as the Christian community feeds on his body and blood, it *becomes* the very life and personality of the risen Christ" (p. 57). Robinson admits, "There is a jump here, from 'feeding on' to 'becoming', which is not explained [by Paul]. And it is a jump not taken by any of the other New Testament writers ...." The explanation, he suggests, is to be found in "the revelation of the resurrection body of Christ [on the Damascus Road], not as an individual, but as the Christian community" (p. 58); again, an over-identification.

The ultimate result of this newly-actualized "solidarity" with Christ—according to Paul's existential realization—and "the new corporeity," as Robinson also calls it, is the *Parousia*, which Robinson then redefines. The *Parousia* is not the "Second Coming" of Christ, but a future time in which the Church, and he hopes the world, as well (suggesting *Universalism*), will achieve ultimate unity and maturity. Thus we become Christ-like, and this world is thereby changed. Such a metaphysical view is friendly to, and presupposes, the *Social Gospel*,

---

[1] John A. T. Robinson, *The Body: A Study in Pauline Theology* (Phila.: The Westminster Press, 1952).

even to the extreme of supporting Liberation Theology such as that of Gustavo Gutiérrez.

Going to Extremes

The theology of Gutiérrez is based largely on socio-political concerns, not on exegesis. That being the case, the Dominican priest from Peru, currently a professor at Notre Dame, is willing to use any hermeneutic which supports class struggle, while ignoring inconvenient interpretations. He is criticized politically for his Marxist and revolutionary leanings, and by Bible scholars for his "relativizing of the Word of God on behalf of political hermeneutics," the "low view of biblical authority" he shares with his cohorts, and his personal view "that a radical revision of what the church has been and what it now is has become necessary,"[1] as well as *Universalism* and redefinitions of Christian concepts and terminology. Gutiérrez considers the Church to ideally represent a "sacrament of universal salvation," facilitating means by which anyone, Christian or not, but in particular the poor, can experience God's grace, enter into Christ, and become the temple of God.[2] As Emilio Nuñez summarizes,

> The church has to be involved in the effort towards world unity because the kingdom of God is already here, and is active in the movements designed to unify mankind. It does not matter if the church loses its own identity in the ecumenical process. After all, in the ecclesiological perspective of liberation theology the church is not an end in itself; it finds its meaning in its capacity to signify the reality of the kingdom of God, which has already begun in history.[3]

Thus we see that a mystical and *existential* view of God, revelation, salvation, and the Church, once divorced from objective use of Scripture, is ethereal, unaccountable, and adaptable not only to Christianity, so called, but to a wide variety of "Christianities" it may serve to jus-

---

[1] Emilio A. Nuñez, "The Church in the Liberation Theology of Gustavo Gutiérrez: Description and Hermeneutical Analysis," p. 174, in D.A. Carson, ed., *Biblical Interpretation and the Church: The Problem of Contextualization* (Nashville: Thomas Nelson, 1984).

[2] Nuñez, 176 f.

[3] *Ibid.*, 179; see also Russell P. Shedd, "Social Justice: Underlying Hermeneutical Issues," in the same volume.

tify—even non-Christian and anti-Christian ones. Moreover, the sac-ramental view, which at base is *Metaphysics*, promises direct com-munion with God: to transcend any number of mundane details of daily life, and petty concerns such as sound doctrine and exegesis, in favor of direct, personal, *existential* experiences of "oneness" with God and ultimate Truth. Having once "released one's burdens," one is free to ascend, in *gnostic* fashion, to a higher plane where one may receive the greater knowledge, the "knowledge of good and evil" of Adam, to become "like God" (*i.e., apotheosis*), and rule in one's own right over lesser, unenlightened human beings.

A Pentecostal (False) Dichotomy

It is now painfully necessary to oppose a fellow Pentecostal, Dr. Howard M. Ervin, late professor at Oral Roberts University, who per-formed such a yeoman's service in challenging, point-by-point, the Conversion-Initiation thesis of James D. G. Dunn.[1] Unfortunately, in countering the deprecation of Pentecostal theology, namely, the Bap-tism in the Holy Spirit as "empowerment for mission" beyond and subsequent to regeneration, Dr. Ervin also chose to frame a false dichotomy between a proper view of spirituality and reliance on propositional truth, that is to say, between Sacramentalism and a mate-rialistic worldview.

In Ervin's economy, two theological worldviews exist: one that is rationalistic, dispensational, metaphysically dualistic, and "procrus-tean" (his word), which considers itself objective and relies on pro-positional truth; and another that is experiential, existential, metaphysi-cally "open," and "numinous" (his word), which is amenable to spiritual perception. This perception includes experiencing Christ sac-ramentally and mystically through the Lord's Supper, as well as Spirit Baptism and *charismata*. Ervin describes having observed "previously nonsacramental Pentecostals/Charismatics [who] have been, in varying degrees, attracted to a sacramental theology as a result of their Pente-costal experience." These Non-Sacramentalists, he suggests, were then "reorient[ed] away from a rationalistic (Platonic!) symbolism" and "an implicit dichotomy between Spirit and matter," toward an

---

[1] See Howard M. Ervin, Conversion-Initiation and the Baptism in the Holy Spirit (Peabody, MA: Hendrickson, 1984).

openness to *existential, metaphysical,* "experiential encounter[s]."[1] (We shall see that Ervin misapprehends Platonism.)

Ervin's dichotomy is so strict that it would not seem unfair to summarize his construction in terms of a clear choice between believing the propositional truth of Scripture and letting go altogether of scriptural authority in order to be spiritual. He states unequivocally, "Sacramentalism and antisacramentalism are essentially two antithetical statements about the nature of reality."[2] He asserts that "sacramental reality" requires that in the Incarnation, "matter itself became a modality of divine presence and redemptive activity in the created order" (introducing the dubious phraseology that "Spirit assumed material form,"[3]—not exactly the same as "come in the flesh" or "born of a woman."). Further, "in a paradigm of a Spirit/matter continuum, water, wine, and bread may indeed become sacramental modalities of the divine presence."[4] In contrast, characterizing the Non-Sacramentalist, "The objective presence and activity of God in His supernatural charisms is either explained away as a dispensational once-and-for-all, or projected into the suprahistorical consciousness of the community, or denied altogether."[5]

Certain facts (to be discussed later) demonstrate this to be a false dichotomy, and a false choice. Moreover, the choices within Ervin's construct represent extremes, whereas a capacious middle ground exists. The Pentecostal Movement did not begin with experience subsequently justified, but with searching the Scriptures to discover how God's Spirit and Christ's Church are meant to work. Others such as John Wesley sought a route to fulfill New Testament expectations, with varying degrees of success; but those who gathered in Topeka, Kansas, January 1, 1901, and many since, having believed the report and received the promise, thereafter discovered the ratifying experience.

---

[1] *Ibid.*, p. 82.
[2] *Ibid.*
[3] *Ibid.*
[4] *Ibid.*, p. 83.
[5] *Ibid.*

Chapter 3. The Intent of the Lord's Supper

The Pentecostal Proposition

Historical, classical Pentecostalism is not at all sacramental; doctrine which can be called sacramental hardly enters into it. From the beginning Jesus began to make objective promises concerning his provision of the *Paraclete*. In John, chapters 14-16, Jesus promises that those who believe in him, love him, and keep his commandments (14:12, 15, 21, 23); who know the Spirit, and in whom the Spirit will come to dwell (14:17); who abide in the Vine, and whom the Lord calls friends (15:4-8, 15), can expect the following objective results:

- They will be enabled to do "greater works than these" (John 14:12)
- The Spirit will "abide with you forever" (14:16)
- The Spirit will dwell "with you, and shall be in you" (14:17)
- The Spirit will "teach you all things" (14:26)
- The Spirit will "bring all things to your remembrance" (14:26)
- The Spirit will "testify of me [Christ]" (15:26)
- The Spirit will "convict the world of sin, righteousness, and judgment" (16:8)
- The Spirit will "guide you into all truth" (16:13)
- The Spirit will "not speak of himself, but whatever He shall hear, He shall speak" (16:13)
- The Spirit will "show you things to come" (16:13)
- The Spirit will "glorify [Christ]" (16:14)
- The Spirit will "receive from [Christ], and show it unto you" (16:14, 15)[1]

Before Christ ascended, He reminded the Disciples of "the Promise of the Father," commanding them to "tarry in the city of Jerusalem" till they are "endued with power from on high" (Lk 24:49). In a more extensive parallel, Acts 1:4-8, Jesus declared this Promise to constitute

---

[1] See lists and comparisons of charismatic gifts in the author's *Christ in Us: the Exalted Christ and the Indwelling of the Holy Spirit* (2007), pp. 156-172. See also discussion of the *Paraclete* promises and gifts in chapters 3 and 10 of the author's *Christ within You: the Indwelling of the Holy Spirit* (Gods Trombone, 2011).

a "baptism" greater than that in water for repentance (*i.e.*, John's), but rather one of empowerment: the "Holy Spirit and fire" prophesied by John (Mt 3:11, Lk 3:16). In "endued" ("clothed") there is no hint of *Sacramental Realism*, but initiation into individual spiritual enablement. Note that we have no "sacrament" of clothing, nor one involving fire (either of which would tend toward formalism and idolatry). There is no "substance" in Holy Spirit Baptism, but raw spiritual power: "enduement" as an analogy describing its instrumentality, and "fire" as a metaphor describing its nature and effect in naturalistic terms.

At no time leading up to Pentecost did Jesus instruct the Disciples to partake of a sacrament in order that they might become "one" with him and experience his Real Presence, nor that by taking a sacrament the "Promise of the Father" would come. At no time during the roughly fifty days before Pentecost is there a record that the Church took a sacrament, not even in the Upper Room. (Their activity, according to Acts 1:14, was prayer and supplication.) Indeed, the idea of experiencing Christ's presence and power *via* sacrament is in direct contradiction to the principles of the *Paraclete* promises: such would represent an "alternative spirituality."

The "Institution" of the Lord's Supper

The Last Supper was in no way an institution of a "means of grace," an alternative means to the indwelling, empowering, and outworking Spirit vested in Spirit Baptism (as if spirituality were "multiple choice").

The Synoptic Gospels and First Corinthians 11 agree that Jesus took the bread, broke it, and identified it with the words, "This is my Body." Only in Luke's and Paul's accounts did He command the Disciples to "Do this in remembrance of me." Then He took the cup and identified it with his blood of the New Covenant. Only in Paul's version did Jesus further command, "Do this, whenever you drink it, in remembrance of me," followed by Paul's explanation, "for ... you proclaim the death of the Lord till He comes" (1 Cor 11:25 f.).

More questions than answers arise from these "words of institution" (so called by Sacramentalists) as well as the surrounding events. The most obvious question is that upon which hinges *Sacramentalism* versus the symbolic memorial view: does Jesus use the bread and wine metaphorically or literally? In short, does the bread and wine literally "become" the body and blood of Jesus, by anyone's definition, and why should anyone think so? Moreover, did Jesus intend for the Church to ever after partake of the emblems with the expectation of activating divine grace or qualifying for grace through the act of doing so?

The Lord's Supper as Passover

As suggested earlier, Jesus' statements would normally be taken figuratively, but Sacramentalists claim this to be a special instance for a special purpose, namely, the institution of substantial "sacraments of grace" as part of the New Covenant. Due to this and related concerns, many Sacramentalists resist the identification of the Last Supper as a Passover meal.

> The most telling points made against the passover origin of the Eucharist are the two facts that the Lord's Supper was held frequently, it was not a yearly feast; and that it exhibited distinctions between rich and poor, impossible at a paschal meal where master and servant sat down together. The textual evidence in favour of the paschal theory is, at first, overwhelming.[1]

Indeed, Paul's version suggests that the Lord's Supper was being "held frequently," at least in Corinth, but is lone witness to any class distinctions, unless one wants to throw into the mix the washing of the Disciples' feet, John 13. John not only does *not* associate the foot washing directly with the Lord's Supper, but does not mention the bread and wine at all. In John's version, taken in isolation, were there any sacramental practice intended to be "instituted," one would presume it to be "foot washing" instead of partaking bread and wine. Moreover, the foot washing appears to be by way of demonstration, in order to convey a principle, in response to the Disciples' personal dispute over "who will be greatest"—which is not, in a demonstrative sense, unlike the purpose of the Communion emblems themselves, *i.e.*, *demonstration*, not *institution*.

---

[1] James Thomson Shotwell, "A Study in the History of the Eucharist," submitted in partial fulfilment of the requirements for the Degree of Ph.D at Columbia University (London: Eyre and Spottiswoode, 1905), p. 32.

In the Last Supper accounts, there is no mention of lamb, bitter herbs, or other standard elements of Passover. If nothing more than customary "table fellowship," however, it was enhanced by a "novel element," namely, the explanations of the bread and wine. If, on the other hand, it was a Passover observance, Jesus would seem to have substituted those explanations for the traditional Passover explanations of the unleavened bread, bitter herbs, etc.[1]

The Timing of the Lord's Supper

Advocates also quibble over the timing of the Supper in relation to Passover tradition. Yet these objections are superficial and—excuse the pun—unsubstantial. Clearly, the Last Supper is a purposeful reflection of Passover. It is without doubt prophetically significant that the Supper and Christ's Crucifixion both coincide with Passover week instead of being associated with the Day of Atonement, which was a fast centered on repentance and substitutionary propitiation for sin. Passover, in contrast, is a feast of celebration, recognizing the blood which marks ("seals") those who have accepted the Covenant by faith and obey its ordinances. One may postulate, further, that the ultimate prophetic fulfillment of the Day of Atonement is yet to come, when the "Lamb for sinners slain," acting as our Great High Priest, having carried his own shed blood into the Most Holy Place, then presents his Church before the Father, "glorious" and "without spot or wrinkle" (Eph 5:27). Meanwhile, those "sealed" for the Kingdom undergo an initiatory baptism in their own Jordan, journeying through their own Wilderness of faith, looking toward their own Promised Land ("rest," Dt 12:10, Heb 3-4 *et al.*), all the time receiving provision from the Rock, the Cloud, and the Bread from Heaven (1 Cor 10:1-4, Jn 6:31 f.). Moreover, a "week of weeks" ("sabbath of sabbaths") after Passover comes the Feast of Weeks (Pentecost), also known as the Feast of Firstfruits, reflected and prophetically fulfilled in the outpouring of Holy Spirit: that Baptism "with fire" providing power to witness and to overcome, as well as all the *Paraclete* promises. Spirit Baptism represents the "Firstfruits of our Inheritance," being a foretaste of the Kingdom yet to come in its fullness.

The demonstrably prophetic timing of the Last Supper, as well as of the Crucifixion and Pentecost, all militate strongly against the sacra-

---

[1] See Klappert, pp. 521 f.

mental view. That view vests spiritual efficacy in objects and/or ritual acts, beyond their clearly prophetic symbolism. Moses' Law specified sacrifices for sin, but those sacrifices "can never take away sins" (Heb 10:4-11, see also Ps 40:6, 50:13). They were not sacraments, possessing in themselves some spiritual efficacy, but pointing symbolically and prophetically to the spiritual future reality of Christ's atoning flesh and blood.

The Lord's Supper as Fellowship and Worship

Then Sacramentalists like to identify every subsequent instance of the "breaking of bread," such as the appearance of the risen Jesus to the men traveling to Emmaus (Lk 24:30) and the fellowship "from house to house" following Pentecost (Acts 2:46) as a sacramental celebration. They even adduce the example of Melchizedek, who "brought out bread and wine" (Gen 14:18), as a prophetic *type*. Such assumptions are tantamount to the sacramental claims already discussed, regarding the bread in John 6 and the wedding at Cana. There was no wine in John 6, no bread at Cana; over-identification of every episode of "breaking bread" as Holy Communion is unwarranted; and no such episode other than Paul mentioned in First Corinthians can be assumed to be anything more than customary "table fellowship."

Table fellowship was a common element of Hebrew hospitality, in which it implied:

> … sharing in Yahweh's blessing. …. The head of the household took the bread and spoke over it the benediction on behalf of all those present…. Then he broke the bread that had been blessed and gave each at the table a piece. In this way every participant in the meal received a share of the benediction. …. Then everyone drank from the cup of blessing, in order to receive a part of the benediction pronounced over the wine.[1]

As to the question whether the Lord's Supper was in fact "held frequently" in the primitive Church, or intended according to Christ's meager instructions to become a regular part of worship rather than an annual observance (perhaps a Christian replacement for Passover or an "enhanced" Passover)—the traditional view and practice cannot be confirmed, however early might be its origin. "The disciples met 'to

---

[1] Klappert, p. 521 f.

break bread, with thanksgiving,' but nowhere is it stated that they met to repeat the ceremony of Christ's last supper," wrote James Thomson Shotwell. "The common phrase 'the breaking of bread,' (η $\kappa\lambda\alpha\sigma\iota\varsigma$ $\tau o\upsilon$ $\alpha\rho\tau o\upsilon$) seems sometimes to have a technical sense, underlying such sentences as that of Paul, 'The bread which we break, is it not the communion of the body of Christ?'; but it does not imply that distinct institution, separate from the meal, consisting of the consecration of bread and wine, which is later known as the Eucharist."[1] Indeed, after the Resurrection,

> Such a [fellowship] meal would be a real "Lord's Supper" as much as any specific repetition of the ceremony which Christ performed at the last supper. And when the apostles had become conscious of the presence of Christ with them after they had come back to Jerusalem, every meal would be like that at Emmaus. Whenever they met to break bread, he would be with them; there would be no need of any memorial when the person commemorated was present.

> Such, as well as we can make out, was the character of the meetings of the early disciples. There could be no regularity nor system, no set rules nor rites to perform. They varied widely in both character and in form as the Spirit came and went. There is no evidence that they repeated Christ's actions in a set ceremony, but might we not surmise that the words of Christ were repeated as part of the formula of blessing?[2]

Percy Gardner wrote, as well, "It was exceedingly natural that in this way every common meal should become a banquet of communion with the risen Lord."[3]

Sacramental Realism Not in Evidence

Shotwell further notes that *The Didache*, dated to the late First or early Second Century, describes in chapters 9 and 10 the rules for the Lord's Day thanksgiving ceremony, yet contains no hint of *Sacramental Realism*:

---

[1] Shotwell, p. 26.

[2] *Ibid.*, p. 27.

[3] Percy Gardner, *Exploratio Evangelica: A Brief Examination of the Basis and Origin of Christian Belief* (NY: G. P. Putnam's Sons, 1899), p. 455.

The Lord's Supper, the "breaking of bread" which is here described, is apparently not a mere rite but a real meal. The expression "after being filled" shows distinctly that this is the case. There is no express repetition of Christ's last supper, and no reference to its prophetic import. But the simple meal itself is transformed into something that bears a close resemblance to it. If it were not for that one phrase, it might have been possible to interpret the rest of the description as implying a repetition of the Last Supper. For the cup and the bread after all suggest, if they do not expressly symbolize, the blood and body of Christ. Yet as it stands there is no memorial of Christ's death.

The main thing, however, in the eyes of our author is the thanksgiving. His whole concern is to teach that proper thanks be given at the breaking of bread. This idea so overshadows all others that he calls the whole ceremony a "Thanksgiving" or "Eucharist." This is the first time we come upon the word used in this wide sense, and it is a strange fact that the first historian of the Eucharist does not describe the Last Supper, our Eucharist, at all![1]

Pliny the Younger's letter to Trajan (10.96-97, A.D. 111-113) likewise makes no mention of a sacramental rite, only a communal meal following a dawn service, at a secondary location. A later installment of this study will feature a review of additional early testimony for or against the sacramental argument.

A Shift from Passover to Communion

The known evidence suggests that the Lord's Supper developed from a Passover observance to a regular practice early on. Certainly some development is reflected in the tradition taught by Paul to the Corinthians. The Synoptic Gospels all portray the Last Supper as a Passover meal,[2] yet it would appear that the expanding Gentile church soon left behind the Passover trappings. That celebration, a vestige of Moses' Law, likely seemed irrelevant and incomprehensible to them. It is hardly sensible, after all, that an initially Christ-centered observance, in particular a purported sacramental rite, would regress toward

---

[1] Shotwell, p. 30.
[2] See Klappert, p. 527.

the Passover theme presented in the Gospels; rather, the other way around.[1]

While the rash claim of Klappert and his sources that the Lord's Supper was "celebrated daily or weekly from the beginning" is unsupported, it would seem to be true that the connection of the Lord's Supper to a Passover celebration was removed very early on.[2]

It has therefore been postulated that early worshippers, in their enthusiasm, combined the fellowship meal theme of the Lord's Supper with the "Love Feast" of the primitive church, adding also the apocalyptic motif of the Lord's "once for all" sacrifice for sin, into one frequent observance.[3]   Still the celebration cannot be shown to have developed a sacramental component or emphasis until a later timeframe.

---

[1] *Ibid.*
[2] *Ibid.*, p. 531.
[3] *Ibid.*, p. 524.

Chapter 4. Sacramentalism Weighed in the Balance

An Absence of Substance until Fulfillment

It is correct, in the prophetic framework of Scripture, to state that all the sacrifices of the Old Covenant prefigure the New Covenant in such a way as to set a paradigm. It is even correct to say, in principle, that the Old Testament, Old-Covenant prefigurement represents the foreshadow of the later spiritual reality and "substance" of the New Covenant (as also the Davidic Kingdom that of the Kingdom of God, and the Davidic kingship that of Messiah, Son of David). But it would *not* be correct to assume that this framework and prefigurement presupposes a substantial, objective fulfillment of all the elements of the New Covenant *before* the final culmination, especially during this intervening time known as the Church Age. The commission of the Twelve and the Seventy to go out two by two and "heal the sick, cleanse the lepers, raise the dead, cast out devils" (Mt 10:8) was not yet the reality of the Pentecostal outpouring to follow. In turn, Pentecost did not fulfill the wonders, signs, "blood, and fire, and vapour of smoke: The sun … turned into darkness, and the moon into blood" (Acts 2:19 f.) of the End-Time. The Kingdom of God which is "drawing nigh," as John first preached, is still in process of drawing nigh.

We still "see through a glass, darkly," "beholding as in a glass the glory of the Lord," but one day "face to face … then shall I know even as also I am known," when we "are changed into the same image from glory to glory, even as by the Spirit of the Lord" (1 Cor 13:12, 2 Cor 3:18). We have not "already attained" nor yet "apprehended" our "completion" in the Lord (Php 3:12-16). Thus one cannot expect concrete reality—literal, ultimate fulfillment—of prophecy before its culmination, certainly not vested in manmade, physical, temporal emblems, nor in the ritual act of partaking them. There is no theological purpose or sense, neither precedent nor parallel, to Christ introducing to the Church a sacramental use of elements in substitution for his Crucifixion either before or after the event itself took place. Biblical prophetic events are never *cyclical*, but strictly *linear*. *Before* the Crucifixion, the observance can only be *prophetic*; *afterward*, only *memorial*.

The 'Presence' Canard and Idolatry

Were Christ present in the bread and wine, one wonders how Christ could have manifested "Real Presence" at the Last Supper, when theologically He was simultaneously "fully human," *i.e.*, fully present in his Incarnation. A few historic teachers actually profess the dubious contrivance that Jesus handled his own body, and even ate it:

> After having spoken thus [at the Last Supper], the Lord rose up from the place where he had made the Passover and had given his body as food and his blood as drink, and he went with his disciples to the place where he was to be arrested. But he ate of his own body and drank of his own blood, while he was pondering on the dead. With his own hands the Lord presented his own body to be eaten, and before he was crucified he gave his blood as drink.[1]

> Christ was carried in his own hands when, referring to his own body, he said, 'This is my body' [Mt 26:26]. For he carried that body in his hands.[2]

Such materialism and literalism tend to produce superstition and ultimately idolatry. When people began to venerate the brazen serpent Moses mounted on a pole (which Jesus identified prophetically with himself, Jn 3:14), Hezekiah had it destroyed (2 Kings 18:4). The sanctuaries at Beth-el, Mizpeh, Shiloh, and Gilgal had to be destroyed, even the Tabernacle itself, due to idolatrous worship. The people were not to put their trust in the Temple, or the Ark of the Covenant, or in God's purported responsibility to defend Jerusalem, but in the invisible God himself. Gideon made himself a trophy ("ephod") which became a "snare" to him and his family (Jdg 8:27). There were to be no objects of veneration, nor idols, for "God is spirit."

The Lord's Supper is not designed as a "concretization" of a spiritual reality, but a "remembrance" (*anamnesis*, "memorial"), for which

---

[1] Aphraahat the Persian Sage, *Treatises* 12:6 (A.D. 340) in "The Fathers of the Church, according to Topic," most selections from "Fathers Know Best" at catholic.com [edited by Br. Sean, a choir monk, 2008], p. 77).
[2] Augustine, *Explanations of the Psalms* 33:1:10 (A.D. 405) in *Ibid.*, p. 78.

Passover was the paradigm (see Ex 12:14 ff.). While the Passover ultimately looked forward to the Atonement, prophetically, like all the other blood sacrifices—the observance itself is a reenactment. Participants reenact Israel's past deliverance from bondage and covering for sin, being sealed with the earnest of blood, anticipating incorporation into future or continued covenant promise. None of the Passover elements are sacramental, in the sense of spiritual presence or efficacy, but have memorial and prophetic significance. Likewise, while the Last Supper looked forward to the Crucifixion, and ultimately the Atonement, the commandment inherent to the Supper's "Do this" is to remember ever after one's deliverance from bondage to sin, sealing by blood sacrifice, with the earnest of the Holy Spirit, anticipating future redemption and incorporation into the Kingdom of promise.

Objective versus Subjective Reality

It was first noted in Chapter 1 that, exegetically speaking, the case for *Sacramental Realism* is an argument from silence, reading into the account of the Last Supper, and Christ's intent by it, a materialistic and sacramental view of the Communion emblems, as opposed to a memorial observance; and an alternate spirituality, as opposed to Biblical Holy Spirit Baptism. Sacramentalists are prone to gloss quickly over exegetical details and make unfounded assertions of reality. In a previous installment, three such cases were reviewed, demonstrating the reliance of Sacramentalists, as well, upon claims of personal experience and what amounts to subjective "special revelation." (Later, we shall review further claims from early Church history and theology.) Such claims tend to divorce *Sacramentalism* and other forms of Mysticism from Scripture and any other objective viewpoint. Ironically, it is claims of spiritual realism which thus threaten to undermine objective reality and revelation. Dr. Ervin's construct, we recall, presented a false choice between spirituality and objective truth.

The actual intent of Jesus was to present a prophetic reality, initially to be fulfilled in the Crucifixion, with an added future (*i.e.*, post-Resurrection) memorial function. The object of this fulfilled "Passover" was to portray initiation of the New Covenant, not through efficacy of the symbolic emblems, but in the real sacrifice of Christ that they represent. The Church, moving forward in the prophetic calendar, being marked for future redemption, would then obtain marvelous provision through the Baptism and gifts of the Holy Spirit, the prophetic fulfillment of the Feast of Pentecost. Thenceforward, the Church has been called to reenact Christ's one-time sacrifice in joyful yet thoughtful recognition, *i.e.*, the Lord's Supper.

Both *Mysticism* and "prophetic reality" are called spiritual, in their respective senses, but prophetic reality is not subjective. Mysticism relies on subjective feelings, metaphysical senses, and *existential* experiences; or rather, claims thereto which cannot be demonstrated, examined, or verified. In stark contrast, prophecy, if genuine, always has an object: a future event scheduled to take place, a promise to be fulfilled, a fate sealed, a fact confirmed, a declaration of truth from the Lord by his Holy Spirit. There is no divide, no dichotomy between prophetic, spiritual reality and propositional truth, either from Scripture or *via* prophetic utterance. God speaks his Word, and it is objective Truth.

The outpouring of the Holy Spirit beginning at Pentecost proves that the spiritual things of God represent propositional, objective truth. God speaks to Joel that He "will pour out of my Spirit upon all flesh." That promise is objective, propositional truth to the prophet: it need not be whiffed, distilled, and reconstituted to be heard. It rings clear as a bell, so that the prophet hears it, comprehends it, remembers it, can write it down on a scroll for all to see. Others can read it centuries later, and know its propositional truth. In God's time, its literal fulfillment takes place: at the third hour of the morning, in the Upper Room, people hear the sound of rushing wind, they see tongues of fire light on each one, some participate, others hear various participants speak in diverse languages. People go and tell others what they have seen and heard, someone writes down what happened, and millennia later, other people read what was written.

(The only thing subjective is whether anyone involved was drunk. In other words, God's Word is objective, prophetic events are objective, historical events are objective, only our perception of those things is subjective. Too many people today live subjectively, by and large; meanwhile, they relativistically doubt objective truth, yet claim to do exactly the opposite.)

To this day, people have the opportunity to receive the propositional truth of the Gospel: to repent, believe in the Lord, call on his name, and receive the gift of the Holy Spirit. "Repent, and be baptized every one of you in the name of Jesus Christ for the remission of sins, and you shall receive the gift of the Holy Spirit: for the promise is unto you, and to your children, and to all that are afar off, even as many as the Lord our God shall call" (Acts 2:38 f.). "You shall receive power, after the Holy Ghost is come upon you" (Acts 1:8). "... on the Gentiles also was poured out the gift of the Holy Ghost: for they heard them speak with tongues, and magnify God" (Acts 10:45 f.). The initial evidence of speaking in tongues, the charismatic "manifestations" of the indwelling Spirit, the "fruit of the Spirit" which are the outward result of spiritual discipline—all objective, visible, capable of being witnessed, examined by others, judged, withheld by the recipient or "quenched" at will (1 Cor 14:29 f., 1 Th 5:19).

Scripture is full of propositional truths that we are expected to believe, obey, and act upon. Acting on what we have received, and objectively believe, is both the exercise and a demonstration of our faith—the exercise of which spawns experience and bears fruit.

Naysayers to Objectivity

It will be objected by partisans that this concern for objective, propositional truth stems from a Modernist conceit that an interpreter can be neutral and that objective truth can be known. Kenneth Archer writes,

> Modernity has always defined objectivity over and against subjectivity and viewed subjectivity as potentially flawed. 'The assumption is that if the biblical text is approached from the stance of human experience, then the interpretation is more subjective; but if approached on the basis of logic and reason, the interpretation is more objective'. The Modernists desire to pretend to be a neutral interpreter by setting aside one's experience and/or presuppositions is a false illusion.[1]

The retort to this presumptive and prejudicial accusation need not resort to a logico-philosophical defense "in kind." Simply, each propositional statement of Scripture—let us specify "the Promise of the Father"—is clearly defined, promised, targeted, scheduled, expected, anticipated; and in time received, experienced, evidenced, witnessed,

---

[1] Kenneth J. Archer, *A Pentecostal Hermeneutic for the Twenty-First Century: Spirit, Scripture and Community* (London: T&T Clark International, 2004), p. 72.

noted, reported, duly recorded, described in writing by definite persons in a definite place and time; its record saved, copied, distributed, protected, handed down, and widely read for two millennia. The modern reader, then, is confronted with the record of the proposition and concomitant, confirming events, which he is equipped neither to prove nor disprove at this point. As a self-contained system, the propositional truth of Scripture is objective, insofar as its original meaning and intent can be understood; only the interpretation and application that the reader chooses to make of it can rightly be called subjective.

The objective nature of propositional truth versus subjectivity is well illustrated by Stanley Harvey, Pentecostal pastor in Sydney, Australia. Comparing ice cream to insulin, Harvey demonstrates that one's choice of ice cream flavors is entirely subjective: there is neither an absolute moral component to flavor preferences, nor harm, nor affront. It reasonably matters to no one else which flavor one chooses. Insulin, on the other hand, is a crucial drug, designed for a specific malady and treatment, with specific dosage, which literally cannot be compromised without dire risk. The properties and proper use of insulin is absolute, and no one's opinion or preference will change them. As Harvey summarizes, "Objective truth is truth for everyone, everywhere because it is based on the object independent of the perception of the observer."[1]

Therefore, Archer's error is to discount Scripture's objective truth within its inherent closed continuum of cause and effect, or rather proposition and realization/confirmation (or in some cases *type* and *antitype*). He confuses objective truth with mundane (subjective) issues of interpretation and the presumption of (subjective) philosophical-worldview bias. Any risk of subjective misinterpretation of the inherently objective material (*e.g.*, Scripture) will stem not from the effort to reconstruct original, intentional meaning from the methodical assembly of "knowns," such as the text itself, word etymology, grammar, syntax, and especially real-world usage; but from destructive methodologies and assumptions based on some external, biased, prejudicial, and even dishonest agenda. In other words, we have the tools today to interpret and exegete well enough, but must guard against the temptation to reinterpret and *eisegete*.

---

[1] Stanley Harvey, "Insulin or Chocolate Ice Cream," posted 8/9/11 at http://blog.-pentecostalsofsydney.com/2011/09/08/insulin-or-chocolate-ice-cream/.

The sacramental worldview, and the sacramental agenda which follows after it, not being ultimately based on Scripture but on claims of *existential* experience, tends to fall into the temptation of such a destructive interpretation of Scripture, or at least a willingness to relax, and other times force, interpretations and applications of Scripture according to its experiential agenda, as it has in the case of the Lord's Supper and its emblems.

A Philosophical 'Line in the Sand'

Experts generally characterize the objective-subjective debate in terms of Platonic philosophy versus Aristotelian and Enlightenment rationalism (more on philosophical origins in this study's final installments). We have already seen the dubious spiritual/propositional dichotomy framed by Howard Ervin.

Father Donald Keefe, a Jesuit, approaches the sacramental question in terms of (theoretical) quantum physics.[1] In particular, he draws a comparison with Heisenberg's "uncertainty principle." According to that theory, it is not possible to calculate both the exact position and the momentum of a quantum particle at the same moment, the assumption being that the very act of close examination will disrupt the system and affect the result. This principle (I read) can also be applied, theoretically, to time, energy, and other relational systems.

Albert Einstein famously rejected the "chaos" represented by this school of quantum thought in favor of a scientific *determinism* (which Keefe calls "a rationality self-enclosed within its own logic"), saying, "God does not play dice."[2] Keefe declares that determinism is damaging to free scientific thought, tending to "suppress the possibility of experimental method." Therefore, "One must then reject the foregoing rationalist dilemma—in which much of the contemporary discussion is locked—according to which one is forced to choose between reality conceived as a jungle, or as a cage."[3] The cage, of course, would represent (restrictive) objective reality; the jungle, utter subjectivity. To Keefe, any school of thought restricted to rationality and absolutes, *i.e.*, "the salvific calculus of those who know"—meanwhile dismissing

---

[1] Donald Keefe, "Faith, Science and Sacramental Realism," in *Institute for Theological Encounter with Science and Technology* (Spring 99, Volume 30 #2).
[2] *Ibid.*, p. 4.
[3] *Ibid.*

"mutability and multiplicity"—represents an "elitist establishment" which he compares to the Communist Party.[1]

Keefe sees a parallel "rationalist dilemma" in the schools of Protestant exegetical thought; while, to the Catholic, the historicity and objectivity of Biblical revelation is "a false problem, one that does not, nor can, arise within the Catholic faith in the Lord of history, for within Catholicism that Lordship is exercised sacramentally, finally Eucharistically."[2] He concludes,

> This celebratory Christian knowledge, this historical faith, this optimism, is more than piety, more than personal faith, more than an idiosyncratic dogma arbitrarily imposed, for it asserts that the objective truth of the world and of humanity is free, because it is given us in Christ. The Catholic faith in Christ is then the free, public response to and the appropriation, at once personal and communal, of the free revelation of the factual, the objective order of reality, to which we have access only by a freedom which is equivalent to worship; the covenantal worship of the Lord of the covenant, the Lord of the history which the covenant in his Blood redeems and orders to our salvation. Only by the praxis of that free commitment do we have access to objectivity. To affirm this is to turn the conventional wisdom on its head, and yet that affirmation alone can underwrite the historical optimism of experimental science.[3]

In other words, as the discerning reader who recognizes double-talk about "freedom" and "objective reality," in particular, will see: "Trust us, we are 'name brand' Christianity, we own the franchise. Base your faith in ritual, in community, in Church history, in dogma, in richness of symbolism, in your emotions. Rest in our arms, we will take care of you. Look no further, take our word for it, pay no attention to the man behind the curtain, don't let the facts confuse you or worry your pretty little head, we know what we're doing."

There you have it, fertile ground for a sacramental religion. The Catholic Church, in the name of intellectual freedom, thus becomes,

---

[1] *Ibid.*, pp. 6, 7.
[2] *Ibid.*, p. 8.
[3] *Ibid.*

via the adherent's despairing surrender to irrationality, "the establish-ment," *i.e.*, to use Keefe's words, "those who know."

Chapter 5. A Convenient Sacramental Hermeneutic

Of course, not every Sacramentalist goes to such lengths as to frame analogies using quantum physics (see Chapter 4).   There are other, more common and longstanding methods of theological argumentation which are more accessible, indeed more automatic, to the proponent. Hopefully, one may presume that the choice of such a non-exegetical or extra-exegetical method is pursued in all earnestness, if not unconsciously.

The Analogy of Faith

Having set aside the historicity and rationality of Biblical revelation in favor of a liturgical and experiential faith, the stage is then set for a sacramental *hermeneutic*: a way of interpreting which is convenient to and favorable for Sacramentalism. Most interpreters who despair of clear exegetical grounds for interpretation and application gravitate naturally toward "the analogy of faith." We encounter this method whenever we hear the phrase, "the general tenor of Scripture," or some similar expression, in comparatively evaluating a text.[1] (I have used it myself.)

Our first step is to obtain an adequate definition of the analogy of faith. Daniel Tappeiner writes, "The analogy of faith is simply an awareness, founded upon observation, of the fundamental unity of the biblical record and the harmony of its parts."[2] H. Wayne Johnson agrees that "the analogy of faith is the harmonious relationship between the teachings of Scripture brought to bear on the exegesis of particular passages," but arguably goes a step beyond in saying, "It is the body of affirmations or doctrines that are considered to be clearly

---

[1] See Tappeiner, p. 51.
[2] *Ibid.*, p. 44.

taught in Scripture and that as a result help inform our interpretation of other passages in the Scriptures."[1]

Properly used, the analogy of faith is predicated "upon the historical-exegetical aspect of the hermeneutical task," never a "substitute" for those objective sources. Its use may be justified only in the absence of clear didactic teaching, to help enlighten "obscure, incidental and figurative passages."[2]

While using the analogy of faith to "inform" interpretation is not inherently suspect, the engagement of "affirmations or doctrines" certainly leaves room for the intrusion of dogma, if not domination by it. Moreover, application of external dogma, tradition, and even superstition, which often stem from interpretive misunderstandings and extra-biblical sourcing, is specious and likely damaging to the process.

Historic Examples

Both Johnson and Tappeiner adduce examples of this analogy of faith principle as used by John Calvin to support his theses and to critique theological opponents, for better or for worse. Calvin, for instance, saw variously throughout Scripture the efficacy of *sola fide*, faith alone, toward salvation, and judged the idea of *Sacramental Realism* to be in contradiction to that principle.

Regardless of one's level of agreement with Calvin on any respective point, negative examples abound throughout church history. Johnson notes that Augustine, while a staunch proponent of Biblical exegesis, alternated between literal and figurative interpretation according to his perception of the rule of faith.[3] Further, Augustine wrote,

> If the sentence is one of command, either forbidding a crime or vice, or enjoining an act of prudence or benevolence, it is not figurative. If, however, it seems to enjoin a crime or vice, or to forbid an act of prudence or benevolence, it is figurative. "Except ye eat the flesh of the Son of man," says Christ, "and drink His

---

[1] H. Wayne Johnson, "The 'Analogy of Faith' and Exegetical Methodology: A Preliminary Discussion on Relationships," *Journal of the Evangelical Theological Society* 31/1 (March 1988), p. 70.

[2] Tappeiner, p. 44.

[3] Johnson, p. 71. See Augustine *De Doctrina Christiana* 3.2.

blood, ye have no life in you." This seems to enjoin a crime or a vice; it is therefore a figure, enjoining that we should have a share in the sufferings of our Lord, and that we should retain a sweet and profitable memory of the fact that His flesh was wounded and crucified for us,[1]

which, by the way, equivocates what modern Sacramentalists purport to be Augustine's position on *Real Presence*, suggesting a symbolic view of the Lord's Supper.

One of the earliest Christian sources, Tertullian, when faced with an unwieldy exegetical argument with heretics, "responded to them not by condemning or exposing erroneous exegesis but by affirming that all of their exegesis was irrelevant because its results contradicted the orthodox analogy of faith."[2]

Clement of Alexandria (c. A.D. 150–c. 215), known for *allegorizing* (figurative interpretation), criticizes his *Gnostic* opponents for "picking out ambiguous phrases" from Scripture, which "they turn ... to their own opinions, plucking a few scattered utterances, without considering what is intended by them, but perverting the bare letter as it stands. For in almost all the passages they employ, you will find how they attend to the words alone, while they change the meaning, neither understanding them as they are spoken, nor even using in their natural sense such extracts as they adduce." He sets forth the interpretive standard of "confirming each thing that is proved according to the Scriptures from similar passages of the Scriptures themselves" (*i.e.*, a systematic study), but adds, "considering what is perfectly fitting and appropriate to the Lord and the Almighty God." In the latter stipulation, Clement accords with Augustine toward making qualitative interpretive value judgments, whether to take a text literally or allegorize it. He goes on to chide his adversaries for "being ignorant of the mysteries of the knowledge of the Church, and incapable of apprehending the grandeur of the truth," having absented themselves from the advantages of official Church dogma and catechism; rather, being "too

---

[1] Augustine *De Doctrina Christiana* 3.16.24, in *A Select Library of Nicene and Post-Nicene Fathers of the Christian Church*, ed. Philip Schaff and Henry Wace (NY: Charles Scribner's Sons, 1892), as downloaded from http://www9.georgetown.edu/-faculty/jod/augustine/ddc3.html.

[2] Johnson, p. 72.

sluggish to penetrate to the bottom of the matter," they presently "laid aside the Scriptures after a superficial reading."[1]

Origen (c. A.D. 184–c. 253), also of the Alexandrian allegorical school, announced his standard practice to be reliance on "the testimony of Holy Scripture," since it stems from divine inspiration.[2] Yet he regards the truth of Scripture as not intended for the casual reader of the literal text to comprehend, but the enlightened. Toward this purpose, "divine wisdom took care that certain stumbling-blocks, or interruptions, to the historical meaning should take place, by the introduction into the midst (of the narrative) of certain impossibilities and incongruities; that in this way the very interruption of the narrative might, as by the interposition of a bolt, present an obstacle to the reader, whereby he might refuse to acknowledge the way which conducts to the ordinary meaning; and being thus excluded and debarred from it, we might be recalled to the beginning of another way, in order that, by entering upon a narrow path, and passing to a loftier and more sublime road, he might lay open the immense breadth of divine wisdom."[3]

To Origen, it does not matter whether specific events literally took place, because

> ... where the historical narrative could not be made appropriate to the spiritual coherence of the occurrences, He inserted sometimes certain things which either did not take place or could not take place; sometimes also what might happen, but what did not: and He does this at one time in a few words, which, taken in their "bodily" meaning, seem incapable of containing truth, and at another by the insertion of many. And this we find frequently to be the case in the legislative portions, where there are many things manifestly useful among the "bodily" precepts, but a very great

---

[1] Clement *Stromata* 16.96, 97 (referred to in Johnson, p. 71 notes), in Fenton John Anthony Hort and Joseph B. Mayor, *Clement of Alexandria: Miscellanies Book VII: the Greek Text with Introduction, Translation, Notes, Dissertations and Indices* (London: Macmillan and Co., 1902), pp. 169, 171, 173.

[2] (Origen *De Principiis* 4.1, in Frederick Crombie, trans., *Ante-Nicene Fathers*, vol. 4, eds. Alexander Roberts, James Donaldson, and A. Cleveland Coxe (Buffalo, NY: Christian Literature Publishing Co., 1885), rev. and ed. for *New Advent* by Kevin Knight, at http://www.newadvent.org/fathers/04124.htm.

[3] *Ibid.*, 4.15.

number also in which no principle of utility is at all discernible, and sometimes even things which are judged to be impossibilities.[1]

Rather, the astute reader "will observe that in those narratives which appear to be literally recorded, there are inserted and interwoven things which cannot be admitted historically, but which may be accepted in a spiritual signification."[2] Yet his readers should not "entertain the suspicion that we do not believe any history in Scripture to be real, because we suspect certain events related in it not to have taken place; or that no precepts of the law are to be taken literally, because we consider certain of them, in which either the nature or possibility of the case so requires, incapable of being observed; or that we do not believe those predictions which were written of the Saviour to have been fulfilled in a manner palpable to the senses; or that His commandments are not to be literally obeyed."[3] What is important is that the Scripture be "allegorically understood.... For, with respect to holy Scripture, our opinion is that the whole of it has a 'spiritual,' but not the whole a 'bodily' meaning, because the bodily meaning is in many places proved to be impossible" (4.20). In sum, "Now all this ... was done by the Holy Spirit in order that, seeing those events which lie on the surface can be neither true nor useful, we may be led to the investigation of that truth which is more deeply concealed, and to the ascertaining of a meaning worthy of God in those Scriptures which we believe to be inspired by Him."[4]

The above examples demonstrate an historic drift, over time, away from the literal meaning of Scripture, and a resort to more convenient, and as Origen suggested, "useful" hermeneutics. Apparently Scripture, under fire from critics and competitors, tended to be increasingly misapprehended, being distant from historical memory and detached in perceived relevance from contemporary life, becoming in many cases offensive to contemporary moral and social sensibilities. Such pressures, and temptations, urged interpreters and defenders of the official apostolic Church away from reliance and trust in the literal meaning and toward alternate approaches. What began with maintaining doctrine, institutions, and practices handed down through *Apostolic Suc-*

---

[1] *Ibid.*

[2] *Ibid.*, 4.16.

[3] *Ibid.*, 4.19.

[4] *Ibid.*, 4.15.

cession became an entrenchment of dogma, liturgy, and ritual, through all of which the interpretation of Scripture would ever-after be filtered. In other words, scriptural agreement would no longer be the measure of the analogy of faith, but the traditions and historical interpretations of the Church.

> Historically, the rule of faith was first identified as the faith confessed by the apostolic Church and considered simultaneously to be the compendium of true Biblical teaching. Later this rule became an ecclesiastical tool with which to control exegesis and guarantee harmonization with Catholic orthodoxy.[1]

> For [Sacramentalists] the analogy of faith is already explicitly founded on the sacramental principle and nothing remains to be said. It should be noted that the analogy of faith in this instance is both the sacramentalist tradition and the "realistic" language of the New Testament. Tradition stands in the place of the historical aspect of the hermeneutical task.[2]

Modern Misuse of the Analogy of Faith

Closer to our time, the Reformation brought a new emphasis on scriptural authority, and presumably a return to Scripture itself as the rule of faith. Yet the Reformer Calvin has already been mentioned as a major figure who adapted and even overruled exegetically-derived conclusions in favor of a systematic view, when deemed appropriate.

Martin Luther has been credited for *sola scriptura*, but his record is not so unequivocal. He derogated the love of philosophy among medieval scholastic theologians, especially the influence of Aristotle. "This defunct pagan [Aristotle] has attained supremacy [in the universities]; [he has] impeded, and almost suppressed, the Scripture of the living God. When I think of this lamentable state of affairs, I cannot avoid believing that the Evil One introduced the study of Aristotle."[3] Luther also rejected the medieval theory of four levels of Bible interpretation, for "if anyone at all were to have power to depart from the pure, simple words and to make inferences and figures of speech wher-

---

[1] Johnson, p. 69 f.

[2] Tappeiner, p. 46.

[3] Daniel P. Fuller, "Biblical Theology and the Analogy of Faith," *International Journal of Frontier Missions* 14:2 (Apr-June 1997): 66.

ever he wished. ... [then] no one could reach any certain conclusions about any article of faith."[1]

Yet Gerhard Ebeling declares that "Luther was no biblicist." Luther favored the Gospel of John, Paul's epistles, 1 John, and 1 Peter above all other books, through which his rule of faith was filtered. Thus we recognize what he meant by Scripture "interpret[ing] itself by passages and places which belong together, and can only be understood by a rule of faith."[2] Because Luther's analogy of faith therefore represented his "subjective preference," writes Daniel Fuller, "the analogy of faith principle does not undergird but undermines the sola scriptura principle."[3] In his emphasis not only on *sola fide* but Christ-centered interpretation, Luther declared, "If adversaries urge Scripture against Christ, we will urge Christ against Scripture."[4] Luther's exegetical limitations and inflexibility are revealed in his failure to resolve James's emphasis on good works subsequent to salvation, versus Paul's on salvation apart from works.

Luther and Calvin both illustrate the potential for abuse of Scripture when the basis of one's analogy of faith is thought "so important that it dictates exegetical method." In such cases, "The choice guarantees that the results of exegesis are in harmony with the analogy of faith. Stated inversely, if the results of a certain exegetical methodology are in conflict with the analogy of faith that methodology must be considered invalid and consequently changed."[5]

> The analogy of faith can be used not only to dictate exegesis but also to replace it entirely. All exegetical discussions regarding context, semantics, syntax, textual issues, etc., are in the case deemed to be irrelevant [compare to Tertullian, above]. The analogy of faith alone is substituted to provide sufficient evidence for a certain interpretation of a passage.[6]

Daniel Tappeiner describes three particular applications of the analogy of faith by, first, a renowned Roman Catholic scholar, and second, in a Catholic commentary. Rudolf Schnackenburg, in the first case,

---

[1] *Ibid.*, p. 65.
[2] *Ibid.*
[3] *Ibid.*, p. 66.
[4] *Ibid.*
[5] Johnson, p. 70.
[6] *Ibid.*, p. 72.

writes in his book, *Baptism in the Thought of St. Paul*, that "the Pauline baptismal texts only allow of being interpreted in a realistic sense"; and furthermore, that Protestants widely agree.[1] Besides the dubious second claim, Paul's passage often considered most "realistic,"[2] that found in Romans 6, far from being clearly sacramental, rather makes the image of water baptism as death and burial *analogous*—not identical—to the process of the believer "reckoning" himself dead to sin (6:11). Because Christ is dead, buried, and raised to newness of life, Paul is saying, we are likewise dead and raised with him: *ergo*, we should choose to act like we are dead to sin in our daily living. As F. F. Bruce summed up Paul's concept, "Be what you are!"[3]

Next, regarding "the washing of regeneration, and renewing of the Holy Spirit" in Titus 3:5, Schnackenburg is equally sure that "Without doubt it serves solely to characterize the saving event that takes place at 'regeneration,' for the primitive Church knew only baptism" (ignoring the "living water" of the Holy Spirit) "as a decisive means of deliverance."[4]

Third, R. J. Foster, also commenting on the Titus passage, recognizes the efficacy of the Holy Spirit toward renewal, yet couches salvation squarely in terms of Baptismal Regeneration.[5]

Tappeiner notes in these examples a strikingly "different understanding of the analogy of faith at work, one founded upon the acceptance of the Sacramental Principle"; and marvels, not once but twice, over the resounding lack of recognition or apparent cognizance or consideration of any alternative interpretive possibilities. On the contrary, the conclusive reality of the sacramental construct is "understood."[6]

This functional or willful blindness to undesirable possibilities is borne out in other defenses of *Sacramental Realism*. In his history of

---

[1] Rudolf Schnackenburg, *Baptism in the Thought of St. Paul* (NY: Herder and Herder, 1964), p. 134; Tappeiner, p. 46.

[2] See Tappeiner, 45 f.

[3] F. F. Bruce, *The Epistles to the Colossians, to Philemon, and to the Ephesians*, The New International Commentary on the New Testament (Grand Rapids: Wm. B. Eerdmans, 1984), pp. 142, 357.

[4] Tappeiner, p. 49.

[5] From Bernard Orchard *et al.*, eds., *A Catholic Commentary on Holy Scripture* [NY: Thomas Nelson & Sons, 1953], p. 925, quoted in *Ibid*.

[6] Tappeiner, p. 49.

the Eucharist, Darwell Stone, an Anglican, compares the "I am" metaphors, including "I am the way" and "I am the true vine," with Jesus' "This is my body" statement, and argues:

> In considering the argument based on these expressions it is important to notice three facts. First, as a matter of interpretation, the explanation that the bread and wine are means, and only means, by which the faithful communicants may spiritually receive Christ is not satisfactory. The alternatives are really two,—"This is in fact My body," or "This represents My body,"—not three,—"This is in fact My body," "This represents My body," "This is a means by the reception of which My body may be spiritually received". Secondly, neither the phrases which are used to support a metaphorical interpretation nor the circumstances in which these phrases were spoken were parallel to the words and circumstances at the institution of the Eucharist. Thirdly, a view by which the phrases are regarded as simply metaphorical attaches to them an altogether inadequate meaning. Each phrase denotes an actual fact about our Lord. It is not by way of metaphor but in spiritual reality that He feeds Christians, and gives them light, and admits them into the Church, and tends them, and affords them access to the Father, and unites them to Himself. In like manner, it is not by way of metaphor but in spiritual reality that the bread and the wine of the Eucharist are His body and His blood.[1]

At the outset, one notes that Stone attempts to dispense with the issue of metaphor in a single paragraph of a two-volume compendious work, which suggests dismissiveness. The question of exact verbal construction he frames is irrelevant: in all cases, Jesus compares an entity with an object, the meaning of which must be gathered from the context. The claim of a "special case"—that being the institution of the sacraments—is inconclusive and represents circular reasoning, besides (since it is only a "special case" if one assumes the sacraments were being instituted). Stone's characterizations of alternate views as "not satisfactory" and "inadequate" are *proleptic* and here unsubstantiated. That Jesus' "This is" statement represents "an actual fact" tends rather to substantiate it as a metaphor, since a metaphor is always a comparative which points to an object, which is unarguably the case in

---

[1] Darwell Stone, *A History of the Doctrine of the Holy Eucharist*, vol. 1 (London: Longmans, Green, and Co., 1909), pp. 19 f.)

the "I am" statements. In sum, Stone's argument, while no doubt entirely sensible to him, is no argument at all.

Similarly, Catholic Rev. R. Keleher considers himself to be in possession of conclusive proof of the sacramental interpretation of John 6. He writes, "These words quoted from the 6th chapter of John are most clearly to be referred to the Eucharist, in which case they prove the Real Presence to a demonstration; from the tenor of the words themselves, they are to be referred to the Eucharist, as likewise from the consent of tradition ..."[1] which, as we have seen, makes appeal to the Catholic analogy of faith, based on dogma and "subjective preference," as well as tradition. He continues,

> He would not thus speak of *being eaten by faith*, or of beliving
> (*sic.*) in his incarnation, which bread, not *He, but his Father*, hath
> already given, as may be learned from verse 32, and which the
> Apostles did already eat, and all who believed in him. That this
> new bread is the Eucharist, is evident from the words *flesh* and
> *blood*, *eating* and *drinking*, so often repeated. Words more
> appropriate, more clear, could not be used to demonstrate the
> Eucharist, which consists in eating and drinking the body and
> blood of Jesus Christ. If the Divine Redeemer at a time
> subsequent, did not institute a Sacrament, under the species of
> bread and wine, we would endeavor, somehow, applying it to his
> death, to eat his flesh and drink his blood, by faith; but when after
> the lapse of some time he instituted the Sacrament of the Eucharist
> in which we so manifestly, so truly eat and drink, it would not
> seem wise forsaking the interpretation which is clear, intelligible
> and easy, to adopt that which is obscure, metaphorical and difficult
> to be conceived in the mind.[2]

Here Keleher appears to *segue* from the John 6 passage directly into the Last Supper, expecting Jesus' statements regarding the Bread of Life to usher theologically (though obviously not in literary terms) into the bread and cup of the Last Supper. Otherwise, his statement that "the Apostles did already eat" the sacrament of bread would be problematic, if not nonsensical. One notes that he seeks no explanation and

---

[1] R. Keleher, *A Dissertation on the Eucharist, wherein Are Proved from Scripture and Tradition, the Real Presence, and the Sacrifice of the Mass* (London: Advertiser Steam Presses, 1872), p. 7.
[2] *Ibid.*, p. 7 f.

has no curiosity regarding the absence of wine in John 6, compared to its unexplained (in that case) introduction into the Last Supper. Keleher makes an apparently unique supposition that had Jesus not instituted the sacraments, believers might have designed their own ceremony. He closes the immediate argument with a rather typical suggestion, as in the case of Father Keefe in Chapter 4, to trust the experts and not worry about such perplexing theological questions.

No doubt many more articles of contention remain on this contentious subject, but the above examples suffice to frame the nature of the sacramental case, and demonstrate the inherent weakness and bias of the sacramental hermeneutic.

Still to Come

The foregoing has in many ways been a *prolegomenon* for what is now to follow. Next, we shall examine the origins of the sacramental philosophy (which indeed it is), and reveal how this extra-biblical philosophy has encroached upon and influenced Christian doctrine and practice.

Chapter 6. Pagan Influence in Church History

What, then, is the source of this sacramental analogy of faith, and Christian Mysticism in general? Certainly, the respective influences of the Mystery Religions and Gnosticism were part of the mix—that could not be otherwise. As Samuel Angus wrote of the Mystery Cults, for instance, "By mortifications, by fasting, by exhilarating music, by self-mutilation, by drugs and stimulants they endeavoured to rise into another state in which they were united with the Deity. To surmount the ills of dualism in union with the Deity or *apotheosis* was their aspiration."[1] "Wherever we find religion, we find mysticism as one of the channels connecting with the Invisible."[2]

However, as shall now be demonstrated, an examination of church history, and the connections involved, reveals that the main stream of sacramental Mysticism, albeit through many twists and turns, flows from Greek (*i.e.*, Pagan) philosophy, principally that of Plato and his followers.

Due to the wealth of information on the personages involved and their complex systems of thought, in order to keep this overview brief (that is, under book length), it will be necessary to forgo detailed descriptions of belief systems and avoid side issues, limiting our focus narrowly to the most pertinent information and connections. The reader is directed to the downloadable companion chart[3] for a grasp of interrelationships. Extraneous background information is readily available to the interested reader from the sources cited and others.

Plato, with a Side of Aristotle

It is commonplace in philosophical circles to this day that nearly everyone's worldview falls into either the Platonic or the Aristotelian

---

[1] Samuel Angus, *The Environment of Early Christianity* (London: Duckworth, 1914; rpt. ed. 1931), p. 93.
[2] *Ibid.*, 119.
[3] See link on p. vi to download the latest version of the chart.

camp. Generally speaking, Aristotle is accounted to have been a *rationalist*, while Plato taught subjectivity and spirituality. In *The Republic*, Plato described a man bound, from birth, in a cave, able to see only the shadows of objects cast on the wall before him, not the objects themselves. Thus Plato imagined the world that men see to be only the shadow of a spiritual or heavenly reality, the world of *forms*: everything in this world is a mere "shadow" of the idea behind it. The real world is the world of thought. It follows from the Platonic world-view that humans are the *shadow*, that is, *image* of God; and further, that material objects such as, say, bread and wine, can also be represented by a greater spiritual reality in heaven (hence *Sacramental Realism*).

To the Platonist, man's soul, created by God and preexistent with him, comes from the world of the *forms*, and longs to return there. Man's salvation ("homecoming") is in "realizing his true nature" and "ascending" back to God; and knowledge is "remembering what the soul once knew." Mysticism is "a search for and experience of immediacy with God. The mystic is not content to know *about* God, he longs for union *with* God."[1]

In spite of obvious conflicts with the Christian revelation, almost from the beginning Plato was accounted by Church Fathers to be "almost" or practically a Christian. Plato's "other-worldliness" commends and is compatible with the ascetic life.[2] Bertrand Russell went so far as to suggest, citing Dean William Inge, that Platonism has been "vital" to the evolution of Christian theology; Christianity is obligated to it, and might well have imploded without it.[3] The "common ground" shared by Platonists and Christians, posits another commentator, is (*Sacramental*) *Realism* and asceticism. "If scholastic in our tendencies, Aristotle may be oftener on our lips; if mystical, Plato; but we overlook their differences."[4] "Aristotle is in the forecourt, and

---

[1] Andrew Louth, *The Origins of the Christian Mystical Tradition: From Plato to Denys*, online ed. (Oxford University Press, 2007), pp. xiii-xiv, 1, 2; see also Angus, *Environ.*, p. 119.

[2] Angus, *Environ.*, p. 184.

[3] William Ralph Inge, *A History of Western Philosophy: And Its Connection with Political and Social Circumstances from the Earliest Times to the Present Day* (NY: Simon and Schuster, 1945), p. 284; see also Louth, pp. xi-xii.

[4] Robert Alfred Vaughan, *Hours with the Mystics: A Contribution to the History of Religious Opinion*, 6th ed., vol. 1 (NY: Charles Scribner's Sons, 1893), p. 130.

through study of him we pass into that inner shrine where the rapt Plato (all but a monk in our eyes) is supposed to exemplify the contemplative life."[1]

Philo of Alexandria (20 B.C.–A.D. 50)

Philo, classed a Middle Platonist (being situated between original Platonists and Neoplatonists), was a devotee of Plato and secondarily the Stoics and Pythagoras. Middle Platonism was mystical in nature, perhaps more so than original Platonism.[2] The Stoics were materialistic and pantheistic, with high regard for reason, virtue, and duty. Stoicism shared with Platonism the denial of worldly passions. Neo-Pythagoreanism placed particular emphasis on mystical revelation and unity with the divine, and couched the supernatural as science.[3] Middle Platonism was also influenced by Aristotle.[4]

As a devout Jew, Philo believed that he could resolve Greek philosophy with Jewish revelation. Most famous is his description of the *Logos* figure, the *ideal man*—a Platonic invention—the *form* in heaven after which mortal man is patterned, but imperfectly. The *Logos* idea, as such, apparently influenced the first chapter of John's Gospel. However, John pointedly asserts that the *Logos* he describes, while indeed preexistent, was no mere prototype but participated in the Godhead and in Creation, then "became flesh and dwelt among us" (1:14) as the incarnate Christ. The concept might also have influenced Paul's "First/Last Adam" concept, though he frames it in reverse (1 Cor. 15:45 ff.). The *Logos* concept, derived from Plato or Philo (or even John's Gospel), went on to influence Neoplatonist doctrines, as well as the Church Fathers.[5] The Fathers took Philo as an example of how "to reconcile Greek philosophy with acceptance of the Hebrew Scrip-

---

[1] *Ibid.*

[2] Louth, p. xii.

[3] See Angus, *Environ.*, pp. 119-121; Russell, p. 322; Charles Bigg, *Neoplatonism* (London: Society for Promoting Christian Knowledge, 1895), p. 305.

[4] Louth, p. 51.

[5] See Russell, p. 289; William Ralph Inge, *The Philosophy of Plotinus*, vol. 2 (London: Longmans, Green and Co., 1918), p. 83; Hans von Campenhausen, *The Fathers of the Greek Church*, trans. Stanley Godman (NY: Pantheon, 1959), p. 31; Louth, p. 68, 74 f., 135.

tures"[1] though his interpretations are often allegorical and even fanciful.

Philo taught mysticism based on contemplation of Scripture ("feeding" upon it as "the soul's food"); through which it is possible, though not guaranteed, to communicate directly with God.[2] Bear in mind that Philo was known for his allegorization of Scripture. Citing the example of Moses' yearning to see God and being allowed to glimpse the "backside" of God's departing "glory" (Exodus 33), God may be approached in "thick darkness," yet is ultimately "unknowable."[3] God is largely known through his displays of power, but the effort to approach him, however far one goes, is joyful and contains its own rewards; Philo describes the approach to God in terms akin to the Mystery Cults.[4] He proposes four types of "ecstasy" which can be achieved through meditation, one of which can be taken literally: the mind temporarily supplanted by the Spirit of God, in which the mind is entirely *displaced*, since human and divine cannot cohabit[5] This form of ecstasy, in Philo's view, describes the spirit in which prophets prophesy, and in no way describes *Mystical Union*.[6] Such displacement more likely concurs with instances of "divine possession" found in Pagan religions.

Ignatius of Antioch (c. A.D. 35 or 50–98 to 117)

Ignatius was a bishop, best know for his letters written to various churches while on his way to martyrdom. Sacramentalists cite Ignatius, among others, as early witnesses to *Sacramental Realism*, by which proponents claim that *Real Presence* was believed and practiced from the beginning of the Church. Ignatius wrote to the Roman church, "I have no taste for corruptible food nor for the pleasures of this life. I desire the bread of God, which is the flesh of Jesus Christ, who was of the seed of David; and for drink I desire his blood, which is love incorruptible" (Romans 7:3); and to Smyrna,

---

[1] Russell, p. 322.
[2] Louth, pp. 27 f.
[3] *Ibid.*, p. 30.
[4] *Ibid.*
[5] *Ibid.*, p. 31.
[6] *Ibid.*, p. 32.

Take note of those who hold heterodox opinions on the grace of Jesus Christ which has come to us, and see how contrary their opinions are to the mind of God.... They abstain from the Eucharist and from prayer because they do not confess that the Eucharist is the flesh of our Savior Jesus Christ, flesh which suffered for our sins and which that Father, in his goodness, raised up again. They who deny the gift of God are perishing in their disputes."[1]

On the surface, Ignatius seems to imply realism; but the most natural interpretation of his use of "bread" and "flesh" in the first passage is as a metaphor for receiving spiritual life, in contrast to "this life." To say that actual bread and flesh brings spiritual life would be presuming on the text; it is rather identification with spiritual sustenance from Christ, metaphorically compared to bread and meat. (This passage has more affinity with the latter part of John 6 than with the Last Supper.) His reference to blood as love is generalized and therefore vague, disconnected from any sacramental reference to propitiation for sin. In the second passage, the issue is heterodoxy in regard to grace, related somehow to a denial of and abstention from the Eucharistic ceremony. The point of dispute is unclear except for connecting the Eucharistic bread to Christ's flesh (note: not also the wine as Christ's blood, not mentioned). Is it clear, then, that the abstainers are disputing the realism of the elements?

The best answer seems to be the following: the dispute centers on "the grace of Jesus Christ" in dying on the cross and being "raised up again." The combination of these acts constitutes "the gift of God" which the disputants deny, so that they are "perishing" in unbelief. By virtue of denying the Gospel, they "do not confess" Christ giving his flesh, and consequently "abstain" from both "prayer" and the Eucharist, considering both ineffectual.

Moreover, during this period Christians were dealing with various *Docetists*, including *Gnostics*, who denied that Christ had "come in the flesh" (see 1 Jn 4:2 f., 2 Jn 1:7). "The greatest heresy that faced Ignatius was Docetism."[2] Many of the Fathers thus deemed it necessary to

---

[1] *Smyrnaeans* 6:2–7:1, in "The Fathers of the Church," p. 75.

[2] Thomas G. Weinandy, "Ignatius of Antioch (d. circa 107/110)" at http://www.-thetruthdecoded.org.au/Ignatius-of-Antioch.php.

emphasize references to Christ's flesh as being effectual toward salvation, as opposed to the *docetic* view.

Justin Martyr (c. 105–c. 165)

Justin was neither raised a Christian nor did he serve any ecclesiastical office (except perhaps deacon in the local assembly, *I Apol.* 65), yet tends to be credited with mainstream Early Church status because of his early date and compelling, principled martyrdom. In his youth, he made the rounds of several philosophical schools, including Stoic, Pythagorean, and Platonist. One by one, he found deficiencies in them and abandoned them, finally hearing the Gospel and converting to Christianity; yet never entirely left Platonism behind, and continued to syncretize select ideas and methodologies of Pagan origin into his own belief system. For instance, he adopted the Stoic principle of the *seminal word*, "the claim that 'all writers, through the engrafted (*emphyton*) seed of the Word which was planted in them were able to see the truth darkly' (*II Apol.* xiii.5, *cf.* viii.1)."[1]

Justin considered that certain Pagan philosophers, Plato in particular, were "schoolmasters to bring us to Christ,"[2] and that both Pagans and Christians can "have a part in the Logos, partially disseminated among men and wholly manifest in Jesus Christ (I, v, 4; I, xlvi; II, viii; II, xiii, 5, 6). The idea developed in all these passages is given in the Stoic form .... For the Stoics the seminal Word (*logos spermatikos*) is the form of every being ...."[3] To Justin, "those who lived reasonably are Christians, even though they have been thought atheists; as, among the Greeks, Socrates and Heraclitus, and men like them" (*I Apol.* 26). Justin considered himself a Platonist as well as a Christian,[4] and set himself up to teach as a Christian philosopher, first at Ephesus, then at Rome, where Tatian was one of his students.

---

[1] John P. Keenan, *The Wisdom of James: Parallels with Mahāyāna Buddhism* (Mahwah, NJ: The Newman Press, 2005), p. 198, note 79.
[2] James E. Kiefer, "Justin Martyr, Philosopher, Apologist, and Martyr," Biographical Sketches of Memorable Christians of the Past (Society of Archbishop Justus), at http://justus.anglican.org/resources/bio/175.html.
[3] "St. Justin Martyr" in *Catholic Encyclopedia* at http://www.newadvent.org/-cathen/08580c.htm)
[4] Von Camp., p. 14.

Justin's *First Apology*, chapter 66, is cited by Sacramentalists as proof that the Early Church practiced *Sacramental Realism*. In the Eucharist ceremony Justin describes in *I Apology* 65, the bread and wine are blessed by the "president" of the ceremony, and then distributed to members—which amounts to that "table blessing" and "table fellowship," likewise Thanksgiving in *The Didache*, earlier discussed in Chapters 1 and 3 of this series. So in the sense of fellowship and individual identification with the formal act of Thanksgiving, the participants are "nourished" by the elements, as well as physically nourished by partaking bread and wine. In Chapter 66, Justin wrote,

> For not as common bread and common drink do we receive these; but in like manner as Jesus Christ our Saviour, having been made flesh by the Word of God, had both flesh and blood for our salvation, so likewise have we been taught that the food which is blessed by the prayer of His word, and from which our blood and flesh by transmutation are nourished, is the flesh and blood of that Jesus who was made flesh. For the apostles, in the memoirs composed by them, which are called Gospels, have thus delivered unto us what was enjoined upon them; that Jesus took bread, and when He had given thanks, said, "This do ye in remembrance of Me, this is My body;" and that, after the same manner, having taken the cup and given thanks, He said, "This is My blood;" and gave it to them alone.[1]

The statement, then, begins with blessing and Thanksgiving, and ends with Christ's enjoinder of future remembrance, leaving only questions raised by the middle part. "Transmutation" ($\mu\epsilon\tau\alpha\beta\alpha\lambda\dot{\eta}\nu$) sounds technical but simply means "change," usually "changing one's mind," as in Acts 28:6. The translation "*by* transmutation" is misleading, there being no instrumental sense present, either in the preceding preposition $\kappa\alpha\tau\alpha$ or the compounded $\mu\epsilon\tau\alpha$-; rather, the suggestion of "change" which accompanies or is an after-effect—not necessarily of the "flesh [not 'bread'] and blood" immediately preceding as well as following—but with reference to the Thanksgiving just made for the gift of Christ's own flesh and blood (that is, on the cross). The nature of the change, which is applied not to the elements but to our own flesh and blood, is most naturally explained with reference to

[1] Philip Schaff, *The Apostolic Fathers with Justin Martyr and Irenaeus*, vol. 1 (Christian Classics Ethereal Library, 1885), p. 495.

believers having been translated into the Kingdom through faith in the Christ whose sacrifice the Lord's Supper commemorates. (Believers now await the literal change of the fullness of the eschatological Kingdom yet to come, when we will be "changed into his likeness," Rom 6:5, 1 Cor 15:51 f., 1 Jn 3:2).

If Justin envisions any realism here, presumably a product of his Platonism, it is not explicit; it is more clear that he sees an immediate parallel relationship, which he and some later Fathers appear to conflate, between the act of being physically nourished by the literal bread and wine of the Lord's Supper, and being spiritually "fed" Eternal Life through faith in the sacrifice which those elements symbolize.

Clement of Alexandria (c. 150–c. 215)

Titus Flavius Clemens was a convert to Christianity, trained in Greek philosophy, Plato and the Stoics in particular, who became a teacher in Alexandria. As we saw earlier in Chapter 5, Clement was an active opponent of the Gnostics but, like Origen after him, was known for allegorizing Scripture. Like Justin, he considered select philosophers to be "pioneers of the truth which was revealed in Christ."

> No people was ever utterly forsaken by Providence, and ultimately "the one true God is the sole author of all beauty, whether it is Hellenic or whether it is ours" (*Strom.* I, 28). The fact that many "weeds" are to be found in the philosophers, as distinct from the Bible, and that "not all nuts are edible" (*Strom.* I, 7, 3) does not affect this fundamental insight.[1]

In John von Mosheim's estimation,

> Clement had vast learning, a lively imagination, great fluency, considerable discrimination, and was a bold and independent speculator. That he had true piety, and held the essential truths of the Gospel, is admitted by all; but no one of the fathers, except Origen, has been more censured in modern times, for an excessive attachment to philosophy or metaphysical theology. He was a true Eclectic, which he also professed to be; that is, he followed no master implicitly, but examined and judged for himself. Yet his

---

[1] Von Camp., p. 33.

education and the atmosphere in which he lived, led him to lean towards Platonism and Stoicism. His great error was, that he overrated the value of philosophy or human reason, as a guide in matters of religion. He also indulged his imagination, as all the learned of his age did, to excess; and construed the Bible allegorically, and fancifully.[1]

To Clement, the ideal Christian was the *Perfect Gnostic*, not in the same sense as the Gnostics the Church opposed, but as the perfect blend of love and knowledge. The Perfect Gnostic is "in the world but not of it," without hindrance or foible, neither frightened nor allured by the world, needing no human teacher, his life an unending prayer, his relationship with God a "constant feast."[2] Such a person wishes to be "free of all limitations"[3] which, as we shall see, is a primary motivation for the Mystic.

> By loving God, the love of God lives in him; he becomes the living, active image of Christ and descends with joy to his fellow men who are all like him called to the Highest and are to enter the kingdom of divine knowledge through him.[4]

At the same time, Vaughan notes, Clement spoke out against "the Montanist type of mysticism," which anticipated "fresh outpourings of the Spirit" to "inspire fresh companies of prophets to ordain ritual, to confute heresy, to organize and modify the Church according to the changing necessities of each period." We have sufficient information in Scripture, in Clement's view, which men of reason can interpret—allegorically—supplying insight to apply to every need. "The presence of the Spirit with us is a part of the ordinary law of the economy under which we live," Vaughan summarizes. "It is designed, that the supernatural shall gradually vindicate itself as the natural, in proportion as our nature is restored to its allegiance to God," which sounds like John A. T. Robinson's version of the *Parousia*, and Gutiérrez' version of the Church (see Chapter 2). "It is not necessary that we should be inspired in the same way as the sacred writers were, before

---

[1] John Lawrence von Mosheim, *Institutes of Ecclesiastical History, Ancient and Modern*, trans. James Murdock, vol. 1 (NY: Harper & Brothers, 1839), pp. 121 f., note.
[2] Von Camp., pp. 34 f., 37.
[3] Louth, p. 44.
[4] Van Camp., p. 37.

their writings can be adequately serviceable to us."[1] Thus the interpretive authority of the Church supplanted living revelation by the Spirit.

Sacramentalists eagerly quote Clement *Paedagogus* 1.6, "'Eat ye my flesh,' He says, 'and drink my blood.' Such is the suitable food which the Lord ministers, and He offers His flesh and pours forth His blood, and nothing is wanting for the children's growth," in support of *Sacramental Realism*, but they neglect to include, nearby in the same passage, "Elsewhere the Lord, in the Gospel according to John, brought this out by *symbols*, when He said: 'Eat ye my flesh, and drink my blood;' describing distinctly by *metaphor* the drinkable properties of faith and the promise, by means of which the Church, *like* a human being consisting of many members, is refreshed and grows, is welded together and compacted of both,—of faith, which is the body, and of hope, which is the soul; as also the Lord of flesh and blood" (italics mine).[2]

Tertullian (c. 160–c. 220)

The influences on Tertullian, other than Montanus (a heretic) and Irenaeus (a "rule of faith" traditionalist), are largely a mystery. He was a maverick. Yet he must be included in this discussion because of his pivotal position as "the father of Roman Catholic sacramental theology."[3] Scholarship in general agrees that he established the term "sacrament" to describe Water Baptism and the Communion elements, and was the first to apply the word "mystery" to the sacraments.[4] His student, Cyprian of Carthage, went on to advance the concepts of *Sacerdotalism* and *Sacramental Realism*.[5]

Tertullian was materialistic and realistic to an extreme, considering even God and the soul to be material.[6] Therefore, it is no surprise when he writes, "The flesh, indeed, is washed, in order that the soul

---

[1] Vaughan, vol. 1, p. 286.

[2] William Wilson, trans., *The Writings of Clement of Alexandria*, vol. 1, Ante-Nicene Christian Library, ed. Alexander Roberts and James Donaldson, vol. 4 (Edinburgh: T. & T. Clark, 1867), also quoted in part in "Fathers," p. 76.

[3] Darius Jankiewicz, "Sacramental Theology and Ecclesiastical Authority," *Andrews University Seminary Studies* 42, No. 2 (2004), p. 363.

[4] *Ibid.*, p. 362 f.

[5] *Ibid.*, pp. 363, 372.

[6] Inge, *TPOP*, vol. 2, p. vii; "Tertullian" in *CE* at http://www.newadvent.org/cathen/-14520c.htm.

may be cleansed; the flesh is anointed, that the soul may be consecrated; the flesh is signed (with the cross), that the soul too may be
fortified; the flesh is shadowed with the imposition of hands, that the
soul also may be illuminated by the Spirit; the flesh feeds on the body
and blood of Christ, that the soul likewise may fatten on its God"[1]
equating physical acts directly with their spiritual counterparts. So one
observes that Tertullian was impressed by the visible nature of sacramental representations, as he describes. Furthermore, much of his
"realistic" expression may be attributed, as in the case of Ignatius,
Irenaeus, and others, to the Gnostic and *docetic* controversies in which
heretical forces denied the physical Christ whom the physical emblems, bread and wine, represent.

Plotinus (c. 204–270)

Plotinus was a student of Alexandrian Pagan philosopher Ammonius
Saccas, regarded by many to be the founder of Neoplatonism,[2] and
whose other notable students included Cassius Longinus, Heracles the
Christian, and another Christian named Origen (of which, more to follow). Plotinus considered himself a teacher and interpreter of Platonism.[3]   Plato was Scripture to Plotinus.[4]   Augustine posited that
"Plato lived again" in Plotinus; had he "changed a few words and
phrases," he might have been Christian.[5] It was through Plotinus that
the medieval world knew Plato, that his teachings have been interpreted and "clarified," and that Judaism and Islam as well as Christianity (*esp.* Catholic) have been influenced and defined.[6]

Plotinus' works were compiled by his *protégé* and executor, Porphyry, who arranged them in six groups of roughly nine treatises each.
Hence, they are referred to as *Enneads.*[7] It is supposed by some that

---

[1] "On the Resurrection of the Flesh," in *CE* at http://www.newadvent.org/fathers/-
0316.htm.
[2] Russell, p. 287.
[3] "Plotinus" in the *Stanford Encyclopedia of Philosophy*, online at http://plato.stan-
ford.edu/entries/plotinus/.
[4] Louth, p. 36.
[5] Russell, p. 285.
[6] "Plot." in *SEP*; Russell, pp. 285 f.
[7] "Plot." in *SEP*; Louth, p. 35.

Porphyry's Pythagorean affinities might have thereafter influenced his school in a "more supernaturalist" direction.[1]

Plotinus postulated a divine trinity of "The One," "Spirit" (*nous*, "mind"), and "Soul." (Following Plato, Neoplatonists had an affinity for *triads*, which they increasingly tended to multiply). These entities, or one might better say, "attributes" (principles or *hypostases*),[2] range from higher to lower in the order listed. "The One" is variously called God or "the Good" yet transcends "the Good" and "the Beautiful," permeates all things but is not properly "the All"—transcends "the All," is everywhere and nowhere, cannot be defined, is unknowable and not immanent.[3] "The One" takes no thought of our existence.[4] "The external world is none other than the thought of God transmuted into vital law," writes Bigg. "What we cognize or recognize therein are the traces, imitations, shadows of intelligence":[5] "... existence, according to Plotinus, is thought...."[6]

On the other hand,

> The God whom Plotinus mainly worships—the Spirit—is transcendent as well as immanent in the world of Soul, but purely immanent in his own world, Yonder. In that world He is no longer an object but an atmosphere. The ineffable Godhead above God is of course supra-personal. There is therefore, in the Plotinian mysticism, none of that deep personal loyalty, none of that intimate dialogue between soul and soul, none of that passion of love resembling often too closely in its expression the earthly love of the sexes which are so prominent in later mystical literature.[7]

> The Great Spirit, as the manifestation of the ineffable Godhead in all its attributes, is the God of Neoplatonism. This fact is obscured both by the completeness with which it is divested of all anthropomorphic attributes, and by the mystical craving for union with the Godhead itself, which has been commonly supposed to be the

---

[1] Russell, p. 287.
[2] Louth, p. 36.
[3] *Ibid.*; Russell, p. 288; Bigg, pp. 209, 220.
[4] Russell, p. 288; Louth, p. 46; Angus, *Environ.*, p. 192.
[5] Bigg, p. 206.
[6] *Ibid.*, p. 209.
[7] Inge, *TPOP*, vol. 2, pp. 160 f.

starting-point and the goal of this philosophy. But it is only as Spirit that the Godhead is known to us as a factor in our lives.[1]

In order for the Soul to commune with the Spirit, according to Dean William Inge, it must make itself passive toward the Spirit, losing individuality and self-consciousness, learning to transcend itself.[2]

To Platonists, all humans were thought to possess a "divine spark."[3] As Plotinus elaborates, the preexistent Soul has fallen from his previous status with the divine, and forgotten whence it originated. Within it finds a natural yearning to return to heaven, "the Fatherland," from which it fell.[4] The Soul requires self-realization and a methodology by which to "progressively raise" itself back "to full awareness of his own divinity."[5] That method involves contemplation, self-abnegation, and extreme introspection.[6] The *ascent* towards "the One" actually involves not moving upward but progressively *inward*.[7] The path of rediscovery necessitates self-purification. This purification (*katharsis*) requires "cutting away" every attachment to the material realm that has "sullied" the soul and caused its fall.[8] This process includes pursuing "purificatory virtues," writes Louth, but not necessarily "civic virtues" which would continue the Soul's attachment to material values.[9] This purification procedure is echoed today in much modern psychotherapy and "self-help" teaching, and bears a strong resemblance to the Scientology concept of "getting clear," and tenets of other religions which entail "laying down" one's "burden." "In ascending to Spirit, the Soul loses itself in order to find itself again."[10]

Plotinus describes this "cutting away" in terms of self-grooming:

> But what must we do? How lies the path? How come to vision of the inaccessible Beauty, dwelling as if in consecrated precincts,

---

[1] *Ibid.*, p. 82.

[2] *Ibid.*, pp. 89 f.

[3] Lazar Puhalo, "The 'External Philosophy': The Fathers and Platonism," in *Clarion Journal*, p. 6, downloaded from http://www.clarion-journal.com/files/platon.pdf.

[4] Louth, pp. 35, 40.

[5] Puhalo, p. 6.

[6] Louth, pp. 36, 39.

[7] Louth, p. 39.

[8] Russell, p. 290; Louth, pp. 41 ff.

[9] Louth, pp. 42 f.

[10] Inge, *TPOP*, vol. 2, p. 83.

apart from the common ways where all may see, even the profane? ....

"Let us flee then to the beloved Fatherland": this is the soundest counsel. But what is this flight? How are we to gain the open sea? ...

The Fatherland to us is There whence we have come, and There is The Father.

What then is our course, what the manner of our flight? ...

And this inner vision, what is its operation? ....

Withdraw into yourself and look. And if you do not find yourself beautiful yet, act as does the creator of a statue that is to be made beautiful:... So do you also: cut away all that is excessive, straighten all that is crooked,... never cease chiselling your statue, until there shall shine out on you from it the godlike splendour of virtue, until you shall see the perfect goodness surely established in the stainless shrine.

When you know that you have become this perfect work, when you are self-gathered in the purity of your being, nothing now remaining that can shatter that inner unity, nothing from without clinging to the authentic man, when you find yourself wholly true to your essential nature,... you are now become very vision: now call up all your confidence, strike forward yet a step—you need a guide no longer—strain, and see. ....

Therefore, first let each become godlike and each beautiful who cares to see God and Beauty. ....[1]

If the foregoing passage projects a tinge of "guided imagery," as we would call it today, consider as well the following exercise:

Let us, then, make a mental picture of our universe: each member shall remain what it is, distinctly apart; yet all is to form, as far as possible, a complete unity so that whatever comes into view shall show as if it were the surface of the orb over all, bringing immediately with it the vision....

---

[1] *Enneads* I.6.8-9, in Stephen MacKenna, *Plotinus: The Ethical Treatises* (London: Philip Lee Warner, 1917), p. 87 f., also quoted in part in Louth, p. 39 f.

Bring this vision actually before your sight, so that there shall be in your mind the gleaming representation of a sphere, a picture holding all the things of the universe moving or in repose or (as in reality) some at rest, some in motion. Keep this sphere before you, and from it imagine another, a sphere stripped of magnitude and of spatial differences; cast out your inborn sense of Matter, taking care not merely to attenuate it: call on God, maker of the sphere whose image you now hold, and pray Him to enter. And may He come bringing His own Universe with all the Gods that dwell in it—He who is the one God and all the gods, where each is all, blending into a unity, distinct in powers but all one god in virtue of that one divine power of many facets.[1]

Plotinus goes on to describe his personal ecstatic, transcendental experiences:

Many times it has happened: Lifted out of the body into myself; becoming external to all other things and self-encentered; beholding a marvellous beauty; then, more than ever, assured of community with the loftiest order; enacting the noblest life, acquiring identity with the divine; stationing within It by having attained that activity; poised above whatsoever within the Intellectual is less than the Supreme: yet, there comes the moment of descent from intellection to reasoning, and after that sojourn in the divine, I ask myself how it happens that I can now be descending, and how did the soul ever enter into my body, the soul which, even within the body, is the high thing it has shown itself to be,[2]

to which Porphyry attests.[3] Plotinus adds, in *Ennead* VI.9.11, a description of "The man formed by this mingling with the Supreme,"[4] suggesting "spiritual formation."

Modern-day proponents minimize the ecstatic and mystical aspects of Plotinus's *praxis*, denying any occult practice or hypnotism.[5] They prefer to describe transcendent episodes in terms of *mental discipline*,

---

[1] *Enneads* V.8.9, in Stephen MacKenna, *Plotinus: The Divine Mind* (London: The Medici Society, 1926), p. 83, also quoted in Louth, pp. 43 f.
[2] *Enneads* IV.8.1, Stephen MacKenna, *Plotinus: On the Nature of the Soul* (London: The Medici Society, 1924), p. 143; also quoted in part in Louth, p. 47.
[3] Louth, p. 47.
[4] Louth, p. 49.
[5] Inge, *TPOP*, vol. 2, pp. 148, 150, 153, 158.

as does Louth, *e.g.*, "an exercise in intellectual dialectic,"[1] "an exercise in abstraction and concentration,"[2] or "an exercise in introspective understanding of the self."[3].

Origen of Alexandria (c. 185–254)

Origen was also a student of the Pagan philosopher Ammonius Saccas. In attending a Pagan school, he accounted himself to be "spoiling" the philosophers like the Hebrews did the Egyptians in the Exodus.[4] Later, Athanasius criticized Origen, as well as Arius, for their interest in Greek "external" philosophies which bred heresy and idolatry, and lacked power toward Christian transformation.[5]

Origen adopted much of his doctrine from Plato and Plotinus, and has historically been condemned for four main heresies: the preexistence of souls, a non-corporeal final Resurrection, Universalism, and an insistence on Christ having a human nature *before* his Incarnation[6]—all implied by Platonism. Following Plotinus, the *ascent* to "the One" became seeking after knowledge and communion with God through the Soul's union with Christ as Spirit.[7] The ascent involved three successive stages (note another *triad*): seeking virtue (as in Plotinus' "purificatory virtues"), eschewing material values (as in *katharsis*), and contemplating God (*enoptike*, "metaphysics").[8] Origen supported this procedure using the *Exodus* as an analogy of conversion, the *Book of Proverbs* to define virtues, and an allegorical interpretation of the *Song of Solomon* to represent the pursuit of mystical communion.[9] Further, Origen, like his countryman Philo before him, casts the episode of Moses glimpsing God from the cleft in the rock as an example of God revealing himself to the Mystic.[10]

---

[1] Louth, p. 43.
[2] *Ibid.*, p. 44.
[3] *Ibid.*, p. 36; see also Inge's descriptions in *TPOP*, vol. 2, pp. 149-154, 161.
[4] *Ibid.*, p. 53.
[5] Puhalo, p. 2.
[6] Russell, p. 327.
[7] *Cf.* Louth, p. 52.
[8] See above and Louth, p. 57.
[9] Louth, pp. 53-57.
[10] *Ibid.*, p. 61.

Origen's goal is not only to know God but be known by him and receive thereby a share in his divine nature: thus "divinization," *i.e.*, *theopoiesis* (*lit.* "god-making").[1]

Origen's doctrine, popular among the Eastern monks, later became widespread in the West due to their translation into Latin by Rufinus, though opposed by Epiphanius and Jerome.[2]

Porphyry of Tyre (c. 234–c. 305)

Porphyry, also called *Malchus* ("king"), was the *protégé* of Plotinus, who called him a "poet, philosopher, and priest."[3] Described by Augustine as "the most learned of philosophers," Porphyry wrote a highly regarded treatise on Aristotelian logic, among other works.[4] He also wrote a multi-volume work in opposition to Christianity, which is no longer extant.[5] He is rumored to have been a Christian at one time, and claimed to have once met Origen.[6] Marius Victorinus and Augustine are thought to have understood Plotinus *via* Porphyry.[7]

As mentioned earlier, Porphyry compiled Plotinus's *Enneads*, and Porphyry's own Pythagorean bent might have nuanced those works more toward the supernatural.[8] He also practiced Mithraism.[9]

Porphyry was an extreme ascetic, superstitious and prone to demonic fears. "He was a man of sombre, melancholy mood, and he was a fanatic. The austerest puritan would stand aghast at the severity of Porphyry's morality. His treatise on Abstinence is directed not to men of the world they are past praying for but to philosophers. .... All pleasure is abominable. Horseracing, the theatre, dancing, marriage, and muttonchops are equally accursed. Those who indulge in these

---

[1] *Ibid.*, pp. 71 f.
[2] Mosheim, vol. 1, pp. 275 f., 349.
[3] Bigg, p. 188.
[4] *Ibid.*, p. 295.
[5] *Ibid.*
[6] *Ibid.*, p. 296.
[7] Louth, p. 146; Angus, p. 240.
[8] "Porphyry" in *SEP* at http://plato.stanford.edu/entries/porphyry/; Louth, p. 35; Russell, p. 287.
[9] Alexander Wilder, trans., *Iamblichos Theurgia, or, the Egyptian Mysteries* (NY: The Metaphysical Publishing Co., 1915), p. 9, note.

things are the servants of devils, not of God."[1] Porphyry "found the New Testament incredible, and took the Arabian Nights as gospel."[2]

In the process of time the philosophical principles on which the system of Plotinus rested are virtually surrendered, little by little, while divination and evocations are practised with increasing credulity, and made the foundation of the most arrogant pretensions. Plotinus declared the possibility of an absolute identification of the divine with the human nature. Here was the broadest basis for mysticism possible. Porphyry retired from this position, took up narrower ground, and qualified the great mystical principle of his master. He contended that in the union which takes place in ecstasy, we still retain the consciousness of personality. Iamblichus, the most superstitious of all in practice, diminished the real principle of mysticism still farther in theory.[3]

Iamblichus of Chalcis (c. 245–c. 325)

"Why, O why," said his disciples to him on one occasion, "dost thou grudge us the more perfect wisdom?" They had been told that, when Iamblichus said his prayers, he was lifted to a height of ten cubits from the ground. This "more perfect wisdom," far more precious than dull mathematics or hazy Ideas, came from the Brahmins to Apollonius, from him to Iamblichus,—and from him to our modern mediums.[4]

Iamblichus is known as the founder of the "Syrian school" of Neoplatonism.[5] He was a worshipper of the Egyptian state god Serapis,[6] and his philosophy was more influenced by Pythagoras than Plato.[7] Under Iamblichus, Neoplatonism devolved into *Theurgy*: literally, "work of God,"[8] but actually describing practices ("works") in which a mystic practitioner engages, that are designed to "activate God's

---

[1] Bigg, p. 296.
[2] *Ibid.*, p. 299.
[3] Vaughan, vol. 1, pp. 103 f.
[4] Bigg, p. 303.
[5] *Ibid.*
[6] Wilder, p. 9, note.
[7] Bigg, p. 305.
[8] Andrew Itter, "Psuedo-Dionysian Soteriology and Its Transformation of Neoplatonism," *Colloquium* 32/1 (2000), p. 75.

grace."[1] The Theurgist used ritual to appeal to an "occult sympathy between the material elements used and the constitution of the divine."[2]

The material elements become "vehicles of grace" due to their symbolic meaning.[3] One can readily understand how these ideas could be, and have been, applied to a "realistic" view of the Sacraments, *i.e.*, the elements of the Lord's Supper.

Debate continues to rage over the *praxis* of Iamblichus and his successors Maximus of Ephesus and (*via* Syrianus), Proclus; to wit, whether they engaged in "mental exercises"; or, on the other hand, in magic tricks and manipulation of material objects to engage "sympathy" from the gods or—like Simon Magus (Acts 8:9 ff.)—to fool the public and thereby gain wealth and a following. Iamblichus was reported to have at times levitated himself, called up spirits with incantations, and animated lifeless idol statues.[4]

In his work, *De Mysteriis*, which Louth describes as "little else" but magic,[5] Iamblichus describes in detail by what appropriate symbols and incantations one may effectively appeal to the gods. E. R. Dodds calls the work "a manifesto of irrationalism, an assertion that the road to salvation is found not in reason but in ritual."[6] Scholars have quibbled over authorship of *De Mysteriis*, some supposing it to be a summary of the teachings of his school.[7] Regardless, Bigg opined that "Neoplatonist prayers shed some light on what our Lord meant, when He warned His disciples against 'vain repetitions.'"[8]

> Certain sorts of wood and metal were supposed peculiarly appropriate to certain deities. The art of the theurgist consisted partly in ascertaining the virtues of such substances; and it was supposed that statues constructed of a particular combination of materials, correspondent with the tastes and attributes of the deity

---

[1] "Mysticism" in *SEP* at http://plato.stanford.edu/entries/mysticism/.

[2] Louth, p. 159.

[3] *Ibid.*

[4] Bigg, p. 303; "Proclus" in *SEP* at http://plato.stanford.edu/entries/proclus/.

[5] Louth, p. 157.

[6] E. R. Dodds, *The Greeks and the Irrational*, p. 287, quoted by Itter, p. 76.

[7] Thomas Whittaker, *The Neo-Platonists: A Study in the History of Hellenism*, 2nd ed. (London: Cambridge University Press, 1918), p. 134.

[8] Bigg, p. 309.

represented, possessed a mysterious influence attracting the Power in question, and inducing him to take up his residence within the image. Iamblichus lays down this principle of sympathy in the treatise *De Mysteriis*, v. 23, p. 139 (ed. Gale, 1678). Kircher furnishes a description of this statue of Serapis, *Œdip. Ægypt.* i. 139.[1]

Even if "magic" appears to be too strong a word, and presuming the absence of occult supernaturalism, one suspects that Theurgy, and Mysticism in general, is likely born of a dissatisfaction with the mundane progress of living, an impatience with gradual personal development, a certain doubtful "pushiness" of attitude, and a narcissistic desire to delve into mysteries and gain power over the nature of one's existence.

> I would use the term theurgic to characterize the mysticism which claims supernatural powers generally,—works marvels, not like the black art, by help from beneath, but as white magic, by the virtue of talisman or cross, demi-god, angel, or saint. Thus theurgic mysticism is not content, like the theopathetic, with either feeling or proselytising; nor, like the theosophic, with knowing; but it must open for itself a converse with the world of spirits, and win as its prerogative the power of miracle. This broad use of the word makes prominent the fact that a common principle of devotional enchantment lies at the root of all the pretences, both of heathen and of Christian miracle-mongers.[2]

And further, in the same vein:

> It is not difficult to understand how, after a time, … the species of mysticism we have been discussing may pass over into this one. It is the dream of the mystic that he can elaborate from the depth of his own nature the whole promised land of religious truth, and perceive (by special revelation) rising from within, all its green pastures and still waters …. It must be accelerated—drawn up by some strong compelling charm. The doctrine of passivity becomes impossible to some temperaments beyond a certain pass. The enjoyments of the vision or the rapture are too few and far between—could they but be produced at will! Whether the mystic seeks the triumph of superhuman knowledge or that intoxication of

---

[1] Vaughan, vol. 1, p. 73, note.
[2] *Ibid.*, p. 46.

the feeling which is to translate him to the upper world, after a while he craves a sign. Theurgy is the art which brings it. Its appearance is the symptom of failing faith, whether in philosophy or religion. Its glory is the phosphorescence of decay.[1]

Maximus of Ephesus, having already known some theurgic success, became a student of Aedesius, who had succeeded Iamblichus as the leader of his school. His success in divination led Maximus to become an adviser to Emperor Julian the Apostate.[2] Maximus is believed to have been executed by the Emperor Valens for having presumptuously and prematurely divined the identity of the emperor's successor, the usurper Priscus Attalus.[3]

Of Proclus, more to follow.

The First Council of Nicaea (A.D. 325)

The importance of the Council of Nicaea toward this discussion is the fact that while establishing the eternal nature of Christ (against Arianism), it also confirmed the doctrine of creation *ex nihilo*, "out of nothing." This position undermined Platonist views of the preexistence of souls and the idea of returning to God through transcendental contemplation in order to restore a lost Unity with God.[4]

In Louth's view, this capitulation of a Platonist-Neoplatonist fundamental, though at first blush appearing to explode the basis for Mysticism and *Contemplative Prayer*, instead "freed" the church. Abandoning the restrictiveness of the return to Unity *via* transcendence, the Church was now free to pursue the Nicene, post-Athanasian view of the helpless soul requiring grace through Christ's Incarnation. Theologians further developed the nuance that a soul may now be "divinized" (*theopoiesis*) through what today we would call "spiritual formation," *via* the instrumentality of Contemplative Prayer. (Compare, in Pentecostal/Wesleyan Holiness terms, the concept of "praying through" to achieve *Entire Sanctification*.) Consequently, factions within the Church came full circle, back to Neoplatonism and Theurgy; for it transpired that in the Medieval Church that a

---

[1] *Ibid.*, pp. 46 f.
[2] Whittaker, p. 133; Bigg, p. 309.
[3] Whittaker, pp. 133 f.; Bigg, p. 312.
[4] Louth, pp. 73 ff.

... Neo-Platonist element, which acted as a mortal opiate in the East, became a vivifying principle in the West. There the Alexandrian doctrine of Emanation was abandoned, its pantheism nullified or rejected, but its allegorical interpretation, its exaltation, true or false, of the spirit above the letter,—all this was retained, and Platonism and mysticism together created a party in the Church the sworn foes of mere scholastic quibbling, of an arid and lifeless orthodoxy, and at last of the more glaring abuses which had grown up with ecclesiastical pretension.[1]

Moreover, within the Church there developed "a neo-Platonic cosmology," which "mediaeval theologians highly nuanced" ("from the perspective of a theology of creation stressing the *creatio ex nihilo*"); which thereafter formed "the foundation of theological knowledge" and "remained the basic paradigm for understanding the relation between God and the world."[2]

The Cappodocian Fathers (4th C.)

The three bishops who became known as the Cappodocian Fathers included Basil the Great (329 or 330–379), his younger brother Gregory of Nyssa (c. 335–after 394), and their mutual friend Gregory of Nazianzus (329–389).

Basil was the bishop of Cappodocian Caesarea. He shared the ambivalent opinion of many of his contemporaries toward Greek philosophy, being an admirer of Greek culture and in particular the orator Libanius, whom he knew personally, while discouraging dependence on their literature.[3] Early on, Basil was a devotee of Eustathius, a "pioneer of the monastic ideal," from whom he learned that through self-denial came true liberation to approach God.[4] Along with these Neoplatonic metaphysical influences, Basil also harked back to Clement and Origen.[5] He declared himself *agnostic* (*i.e.*, with-

---

[1] Vaughan, vol. 1, p. 132.
[2] Lieven Boeve, "Thinking Sacramental Presence in a Postmodern Context: A Playground for Theological Renewal," in L. Boeve and L. Leijssen, eds., *Sacramental Presence in a Postmodern Context* (Leuven, Belgium: Leuven University Press, 2001), p. 6.
[3] Puhalo, p. 3; von Camp., p. 82.
[4] Von Camp., p. 83.
[5] *Ibid.*

out knowledge) on many theological points he considered moot, wishing to ignore theology and draw the Church toward peace and adoring contemplation of Christ.[1] Yet contrary to his personal aims, Basil found himself continually impelled toward the exercise of church leadership, in times of emergency, a role for which he came to be most admired.

The two Gregories benefited from their association with Basil, and were credited with a measure of his credibility. Gregory Nazianzus was neither a theologian nor an administrator; rather, a skilled and talented orator who was overly dependent on the approbation of a rapt audience, vain, needy, and embittered when rejected.[2] He benefited further from being of the Nicene party, as opposed to Arian, gaining the appointment of Emperor Theodosius to Bishop of Constantinople.[3] Gregory's theology is built on Basil's, but with more emphasis on the work of the Holy Spirit (Origenic influence)[4] as well as the humanity of Christ (against Apollinaris), ideas pointing toward human "divinization" through "association" with Christ.[5] For these efforts, Gregory acquired the appellation, "the theologian," and for his oratory was later called the "Christian Demosthenes."[6]

Basil's brother Gregory became Bishop of Nyssa and later presiding bishop over all of Pontus. He was a strong advocate of the authority of the Church and the priesthood (though not vitally interested in seeking to establish that authority in Scripture), and the first to clearly define the priest's *sacerdotal* function.[7] His friend Gregory of Nazianzus scolded him for marrying Theosebia, a woman of high social status.[8]

Gregory is Nicene and Athanasian in the sense that he took to heart the doctrine of creation *ex nihilo*. His theology otherwise looks back to Plato, Philo, Plotinus, and Origen.[9] He disagrees with Plotinus that the soul was preexistent with God and may return to him; while agreeing with Philo that one may through contemplation approach God, but

---

[1] *Ibid.*, pp. 88 f.
[2] *Ibid.*, pp. 95 f.
[3] *Ibid.*, p. 103.
[4] *Ibid.*, p. 98.
[5] *Ibid.*, p. 106.
[6] *Ibid.*
[7] *Ibid.*, pp. 111 f.
[8] *Ibid.*, p. 109.
[9] Louth, p. 78; von Camp., pp. 109, 112.

in impenetrable darkness, for God is unknowable.[1] Gregory follows Origen in his use of the *Song of Solomon, Proverbs*, Moses' glimpse of God's glory, and other Old Testament texts, allegorically, to describe the *ascent* towards God, as well as perceiving three ways or stages of ascent (a *triad*).[2] The second way of ascent contemplates the Platonic reality of *forms*.[3]

Gregory's mysticism is based on the Incarnation, by virtue of which Christ has reached toward man in love and enabled him by grace to ascend.[4] Following Plotinus, in the first stage of ascent, the soul begins to contemplate and seeks purification; then engages in deep contemplation; then in the third stage, the soul surpasses contemplation to relate directly to God in a union of love.[5] Contemplation is thus a step on the way to *Mystical Union*, not an end in itself.[6]

Yet in Gregory's view, the soul yearns for God, but is never satisfied. The God who lives in impenetrable darkness, in his vastness, cannot truly be known, only approached. The more the seeker knows, the more he wants to know, but the depth of God cannot be plumbed. Thus the contemplative basks in awe of the infinite, in insatiable longing. The soul "has been mortally wounded with the arrow of love" (see below). One is reminded of the definition of "joy" described by C. S. Lewis as a sense of unsatisfied longing. Gregory himself wrote in his *Commentary on the Song* XII,

> The soul, having gone out at the word of her Beloved, looks for Him but does not find Him … In this way, she is in a sense, wounded and beaten because of the frustration of what she had been longing for, now that she thinks that her yearning for the Other cannot be fulfilled or satisfied. But the veil of her grief is removed when she learns that the true satisfaction of her desire consists in continuing to go on with her quest and never ceasing in her ascent, seeing that every fulfilment of her desire continually generates a further desire for the Transcendent. Thus the veil of her despair is torn away and the bride realizes that she will always

---

[1] Louth., pp. 78, 81, 85.
[2] *Ibid.*, pp. 79 ff., 83, 85 f., 87.
[3] *Ibid.*, p. 83.
[4] *Ibid.*, p. 79.
[5] *Ibid.*, pp. 80 f., 85.
[6] *Ibid.*, p. 83.

discover more and more of the incomprehensible and unhoped for beauty of her Spouse throughout all eternity. Thereupon she is torn by an even more urgent longing, and she ... communicates to her Beloved the affections of her heart. For she has received within her God's special dart, she has been wounded to the heart by the barb of faith, she has been mortally wounded by the arrow of love. And God is love,[1]

which apart from being poignant and romantic, lacks a New Testament theological basis: for among other discrepancies, Paul tells us that "now we see through a glass, darkly; but then face to face: now I know in part; but then shall I know even as also I am known" (1 Cor. 13:12); and also John, "it doth not yet appear what we shall be: but we know that, when he shall appear, we shall be like him; for we shall see him as he is" (1 Jn 3:2). It is not given to the Christian, according to the Bible, to approach near to a holy God in our person, nor to be in union with him, until the End, at which time our mortal bodies, which yearn to be delivered from the flesh, will be made immortal, and Christ will reveal himself fully.

Evagrius of Pontus (345–399)

A rising star in the church, patronized by all three of the Cappodocian Fathers, Evagrius declined the bishopric of Alexandria and retreated to live as a monk, finally in Nitria, Egypt, for the last fourteen years of his life. A "thoroughgoing" Origenist, Evagrius was also much under the influence of Basil and Gregory of Nazianzus, and owing to Clement.[2] Indeed, as Louth writes, Evagrius seems to have chosen the most questionable tenets of Origen's philosophy to develop further for himself,[3] for which both he and Origen were condemned as heretics in later councils.[4] Evagrius outlined three ways of the soul (a *triad*), patterned after Origen. In contrast to Gregory of Nyssa, God is knowable and not shrouded in darkness.[5] Only a soul that has transcended the body to achieve *apathy* can pray a transcendent prayer

---

[1] J. Daniélou and H. Musurillo, ed., *From Glory to Glory: Texts from Gregory of Nyssa's Mystical Writings* [Crestwood, NY: St. Vladimir's Press, 1995, pp. 270 f.; also quoted in part in Louth, p. 87)
[2] Louth, pp. 97, 106, 109.
[3] *Ibid.*, pp. 80, 97.
[4] "Evagrius Ponticus" in *CE* at http://www.newadvent.org/cathen/05640a.htm.
[5] Louth., pp. 105 f.

without great risk.[1] Monks and hermits are subject to demonic attack, and war through their devotions.[2] Evagrius compiled a list of eight evil thoughts, precursor to the traditional Seven Deadly Sins.[3]

Evagrius is important for the influence his writings bore, first in the Greek East, later passed on by John Cassian to the Latin West.[4] A copy of a Latin translation by Evagrius of the *Life of Anthony* was owned by the Venerable Bede centuries later.[5]

Augustine of Hippo (354–430)

As a boy, Augustine was exposed to Christianity by his mother Monica, but later experimented with Manichaeism and Neoplatonism, as well as *hedonism*. For thirteen years, he conducted an affair that produced a son. Among his writings, *The City of God* demonstrates that he was familiar with the philosophers Apuleius, Cicero, Livy, Plato, Pliny, Plotinus, Porphyry, Seneca the Younger, and the Christian theologian Tertullian, among others; in another instance, he visits Virgil, as well.[6] His heavy use of Latin sources and "knowledge of Plato [that] is more general than specific"[7] leads scholars to conclude that he read little Greek; rather, his knowledge of Plato was derived from quotations in Cicero and translations of Porphyry and Plotinus published by Marius Victorinus.[8] Victorinus, whom Augustine admired, had been a Pagan rhetorician until converting to Christianity at an advanced age.[9]

In his early writings, "Augustine is in agreement with Plato and Plotinus in his description of the precise relationship of the soul to the body. The former is the source of life for the latter. The soul occupies in Plato a middle position between the real world of ideas and the

---

[1] *Ibid.*, pp. 106, 108.
[2] *Ibid.*, p. 101.
[3] *Ibid.*, p. 102.
[4] *Ibid.*, pp. 72, 127.
[5] Bertram Colgrave and R. A. B. Mynors, *Bede's Ecclesiastical History of the English People* (Oxford: Clarendon Press, 1969), p. xxvi.
[6] Samuel Angus, *The Sources of the First Ten Books of Augustine's De Civitate Dei*, A Thesis Presented to the Faculty of Princeton University for the Degree of Doctor of Philosophy (Princeton, 1906), pp. 14, 59.
[7] *Ibid.*, p. 241.
[8] *Ibid.*, pp. 233, 240 ff.; Louth, p. 146; *contra* Mosheim, vol. 1, p. 321.
[9] Louth, p. 146.

world of appearance to which the body belongs ...."[1] Augustine's thought on the divine nature never outgrew Neoplatonic influences, and his psychology never substantially changed.[2] His concept of *regio dissimilitudinis*, "Place of Unlikeness," passed on to later theologians, comes from Plato, while the process of purification, cutting away, and realizing kinship with the divine[3] is thoroughly Plotinian. In *The City of God* X.14, in particular, Augustine is clearly influenced by Plotinus.[4] *Confessions* III.6.11, "thou wert more inward than the most inward place of my heart and loftier than the highest," echoes the ascent inward to "the One" of Plotinus.[5] Parry notes significant dependence on Plato and Plotinus in *De Ordine*, as well as some influence of Aristotle.[6] Augustine appears to believe in Plato's concept of a "world-soul" which corresponds to the physical world as the individual soul does to the body.[7]

Augustine circumvents *ex nihilo*, in principle, in his roundly Plotinian concept of man as the image of the *Logos*, longing to return to "the One."[8] The first step of his ascent is, of course, *introspection* in order to know one's true self; then the soul learns to love itself; followed by the pursuit of knowing Christ deeply in order to reflect his image, until achieving a spiritual *trinity*,[9] hence *spiritual formation*. Entering oneself is entering the spiritual world, discovering oneself to be a transcendent spiritual being.[10] The depth of Augustine's introspection is unprecedented: Louth estimates his longing for the Fatherland to be greater than that of Plotinus.[11] Beyond this spiritual formation is a higher path of *returning* to touch God in contemplation of God.[12]

---

[1] Thomas Jones Parry, *Augustine's Psychology during his first period of literary Activity with special reference to his relation to Platonism* (Borna-Leipzig: Buchdruckerei Robert Noske, 1913), p. 10.

[2] *Ibid.*, pp. 5 f.

[3] *Ibid.*, p. 41.

[4] Angus, *Sources*, p. 166; see also Louth, p. 134.

[5] Louth, p. 39.

[6] Parry, p. 3.

[7] Parry, p. 10.

[8] Louth, pp. 129 f., 142 f.

[9] *Ibid.*, pp. 143, 146 f.

[10] *Ibid.*, p. 138.

[11] *Ibid.*, pp. 129 f.

[12] *Ibid.*, p. 148.

Augustine recounts, in *Confessions* IX.10.23–5, a very emotional, possibly ecstatic and transcendent experience shared with his mother, Monica: while musing on the glories of heaven, the two of them become swept up in feelings of love and desire for the divine, rising beyond their own souls to the heavens, just touching the divine momentarily then falling away, sighing with ineffable longing and a sense of realization. Augustine described ecstasy as times when the mind is occupied and totally distracted from the bodily senses (*De Genesi ad Litteram* XII.12.25), and supposed such times to be a fore-taste of heaven.[1]

On occasion, Augustine does quibble with the philosophers. He did not believe, with Origen and Pantheism, that *all* souls would in the end return to union with God; rather, he described an early form of Pre-destination.[2] "Platonists are right about God, wrong about gods," in his opinion, and also wrong to reject the Incarnation.[3] In spite of call-ing Porphyry "the most learned of philosophers," he chides him in regard to Theurgy (to which he objected), saying, "Thou didst learn these things, not from Plato, but from thy Chaldaean masters."[4] He is diametrically opposed to the Stoic disdain for human passion, which to Augustine depends on one's motives.[5]

Augustine is often cited in support of *Sacramentalism*. Ambrose (c. 339–397) had followed Tertullian and Cyprian in their assertions of *Sacramental Realism*.[6] As quoted in an earlier chapter, Augustine had spoken in terms of Christ carrying his own body in his hands. Else-where, he spoke in realistic terms, as well. His doctrine was built on that of his forbears just mentioned.[7]

---

[1] *Ibid.*, p. 133.
[2] Steven Kreis, "The Church Fathers: St. Jerome and St. Augustine," Lecture 16 in "Lectures on Ancient and Medieval European History," in The History Guide at http://www.historyguide.org/ancient/lecture16b.html, 2001.
[3] Russell, p. 358; see also Louth, p. 140.
[4] Bigg, pp. 295, 299; see also Inge, *Christian Mysticism: Lectures before Oxford* (NY: Charles Scribner's Sons, 1899), p. 131 f.
[5] Russell, p. 358.
[6] Jankiewicz, pp. 372 f.
[7] Gaylan R. Schmeling, *The Lord's Supper in Augustine and Chemnitz: A Compari-son of Two Fathers of the Church*, submitted to the Faculty of the Graduate School of Nashotah House in partial fulfillment of the requirements for the degree of Master of Sacred Theology, April 1993, p. 3.

While Augustine agreed with his precursors on the issue of the Eucharist as a sacrifice, he refused to affirm the real presence in favor of a more symbolical understanding of the sacrament. The bread and wine, he asserted, were only "signs" or "symbols" of the body of Christ and whoever was part of the one, true church ate and drank this body spiritually.[1]

Augustine actually used the term "sacrament" broadly, considering it a "sacred sign" representing a greater or hidden reality, and applying the term not only to Water Baptism but to exorcism and other rites.[2] He says in *Sermon* 272, "These things, my brothers, are called sacraments for the reason that in them one thing is seen but another is understood. That which is seen has physical appearance, that which is understood has spiritual fruit."[3]

One suspects here an anti-materialistic reaction to the hyper-materialism of Theurgy. Nevertheless, his view of sacraments was heavily influenced by Neoplatonism.[4] Following the Platonic premise of *forms*, objects in the material world can represent a higher reality in heaven. Gaylan Schmeling speculates that "Augustine makes a greater separation between the sign and the reality in the Eucharist than did most of the early fathers, possibly in opposition to the Manichaeans who held exaggerated physical concepts of the presence of Christ," a separation that Schmeling, a Lutheran, considers a "danger" since it suggests a symbolic view.[5] Yet a symbolic view can only be a danger to the (misguided) sacerdotal system, not at all a danger to faith in the atoning sacrifice of Christ for which it stands.

Augustine makes much of the Melchizedek figure, or rather his offering of thanksgiving and fellowship with bread and wine (Gen 14:18), as a *type* of sacramental sacrifice.[6] This obscure figure, who appears in a "cameo" then disappears into history, is ripe for allegory. While Melchizedek was used appropriately as a *type* of Christ by the author of Hebrews, in that he was a priest in his own right, not by human qualifications, the usage which Augustine inherited and

---

[1] Jankiewicz, p. 373.
[2] Schmeling, p. 7.
[3] Quoted in *Ibid*.
[4] *Ibid*.
[5] *Ibid*., p. 7 f.
[6] Schmeling, pp. 3 f.

bequeathed is *eisegetical*, that is, *read into* the text. The bread and wine which Melchizedek provided can hardly be connected with sacrifice, which was always by blood (as Abel, Noah, and Abraham had demonstrated); moreover, there is in the passage *no* act of sacrifice (as in slaying and burning), *no* "institution" of a ritual, *no* prophetic, eschatological, or symbolic identification of the "elements," nor any memorial pronouncements, *i.e.*, nothing to recommend the passage toward *Sacramentalism*—but the bare fact of bread and wine, staples of the Levantine diet and instruments of common hospitality.

Augustine should have realized that neither objects nor methodologies commend us to God. Faulty interpretation of Scripture certainly does not. None of these qualifies for the "Spirit and truth" worship Jesus foretold. Unfortunately, Augustine's influence became widespread in the Western Church, to this day, and served to encourage Monasticism and Mysticism, reintroduce Neoplatonic philosophy, and entrench *Sacramentalism* and sacerdotal religion in the Catholic and Mainline Protestant churches.

Proclus (412–485)

Proclus Lycaeus "Diodochos" ("the Successor") was a student of Syrianus, and succeeded him in directing the theurgic school of Neoplatonism which Iamblichus had headed, a post Proclus held for fifty years. Proclus believed that all gods should be worshipped, underwent initiatory rites into many of the mystery cults, and prayed to the sun at dawn, noon, and sunset every day. He hoped to preserve the old Paganism against the tide of prevalent Christianity. As an interpreter of Plato, Proclus always agreed with his master, Syrianus, often argued with Aristotle, and sometimes disagreed with his forbear, Plotinus. He is regarded as the most important Greek philosopher of late Antiquity, and helped, albeit inadvertently, to plant Neoplatonism squarely within the medieval Church.[1]

> He is the last great name among the Neo-Platonists. He was the most eclectic of them all, perhaps because the most learned and the most systematic. He elaborated the trinity of Plotinus into a suc-

---

[1] "Proclus" in *SEP* at http://plato.stanford.edu/entries/proclus/.

cession of impalpable *Triads*, and surpassed Iamblichus in his devotion to the practice of theurgy.[1]

Proclus was credited with many miracles over the course of his lifetime. Among other manifestations, his loyal student and biographer, Marinus, records that a government official, Rufinus, had seen a halo around Proclus' head.[2]

In his religious practice and divination, Proclus would variously perform sacrifices, read animal entrails, evoke secret divine names, and use such instruments as the *strophalos*, *teetotum* (a sort of spinning top), the "wryneck" (*Ιυνξ*), and the *tripod*.[3] In his writings, three kinds of theurgical practice have been discerned: (a) *hieratic* (priestly) arts, including using prayers and incantations to perform healings and nature miracles, and to animate statues and prompt oracles; (b) *ascent* to touch the divine *via* contemplative prayer and invocations; and (c) *Mystical Union* with "the One" using faith, mystical silence, and "negation" (*apophasis*).[4]

To Proclus, touching the divine and unity with "the One," in contradiction to Plotinus and the Gnostics, is no longer accomplished through a process of acquiring knowledge but quietness and "giving oneself up" to the divine. Theurgic practice is "established by the gods themselves, to make it possible for the human soul to overcome the distance between the mortal and the divine, which cannot be done through increasing philosophical understanding."[5] To Proclus, God is "known only by ecstasy—a God who is the repose he gives—a God of whom the more you deny the more do you affirm."[6]

> After years of austerity and toil, Proclus—the scholar, stored with the opinions of the past, surrounded by the admiration of the present—the astronomer, the geometrician, the philosopher,— learned in the lore of symbols and of oracles, in the rapt utterances of Orpheus and of Zoroaster—an adept in the ritual of invocations

---

[1] Vaughan, vol. 1, p. 105.

[2] Bigg. p. 320; Dominic J. O'Meara, *Platonopolis: Platonic Political Philosophy in Late Antiquity* (Oxford: Clarendon Press, 2003), p. 20.

[3] See Bigg, p. 321; Itter, p. 75; Louth, p. 157; "Proclus" in *SEP*; "IYNX" at http://-www.theoi.com/Nymphe/NympheIynx.html.

[4] "Proclus" in *SEP*.

[5] *Ibid.*; see also Louth, p. 157.

[6] Vaughan, vol. 1, p. 105.

among every people in the world—he, at the close, pronounces Quietism the consummation of the whole, and an unreasoning contemplation, an ecstasy which casts off as an incumbrance all the knowledge so painfully acquired, the bourne of all the journey.[1]

Proclus accepts Plotinus' original *triad* scheme but adds more triads: there is the triad of "rest," "emanation," and "return." Then there is the triad of "the modes of existence," which is "being," "life," and "intelligence."[2] At the same time, Proclus' list of causes (active entities within reality), of which are three: "gods," "intellects," and "souls," appears to be parallel to Plotinus' original triad. Moreover, "The intimate relation between Being, Life, and Intellect is the origin of the basic structure uniting all causes to their effects, namely the relation of immanence, procession and reversion .... This triad has been called the 'triad of triads,' the underlying principle of all triadic structures."[3]

Happiness for the Mystic is acquired through attaining to "theurgic virtues" by which humans may "act with the gods"[4]—which echoes the "purificatory virtues" taught by Plotinus as well as the concept of "spiritual formation."

Proclus links Neoplatonist philosophy with theurgic practice using a system of *cause and effect*. In this system, first, everything is understood to be related to everything else.[5] As mentioned earlier, he sees three types of active causes within reality: gods, intellects, and souls. From such *causes* proceed properties or *emanations* in the form of *effects*, such that:

> Every thing caused abides in, proceeds from, and returns to, its cause.
>
> For if it alone abided, it would in no respect differ from its cause, since it would be without separation and distinction from it. For progression is accompanied with separation. But if it alone proceeded, it would be unconjoined and deprived of sympathy with its cause, having no communication with it whatever. And if it

---

[1] *Ibid.*, pp. 105 f.
[2] Louth, p. 156; see also "Proclus" in *SEP*.
[3] "Proclus" in *SEP*.
[4] *Ibid.*
[5] *Ibid.*

were alone converted, how can that which has not its essence from the cause be essentially converted to that which is foreign to its nature? But if it should abide and proceed, but should not return, how will there be a natural desire to everything of well-being and of good, and an excitation to its generating cause? And if it should proceed and return, but should not abide, how, being separated from its cause, will it hasten to be conjoined with it? .... For every thing which is converted resembles that which is resolved into the nature from which it is essentially divided. It is necessary, therefore, either that it should abide alone, or return alone, or alone proceed, or that the extremes should be bound to each other, or that the medium should be conjoined with each of the extremes, or that all should be conjoined....[1]

In other words (if one may follow what appears to be circular reasoning), every *effect* must depart from its *cause* in order to change its properties, and only due to change does it have impetus to *return* to the particular *cause* which it resembles; moreover, each *effect* is attracted to that initial *cause* to which, due to change, it is now partially *unlike*. At the same time, his "law of mean terms" in *Elem. Theol.* 28 states that effects which are *somewhat unlike*, i.e., mixed, are re-attracted to their initial cause prior to any effect which is *entirely* unlike it, with which effect the cause has no "sympathy." "Moreover, it is necessary that the thing caused should participate of its cause, as from thence deriving its essence."[2]

To add to the complexity, everything has (a) an essence which expresses its character; (b) a relationship to its higher cause; and (c) possibly also its own subordinate effects—such that "the higher a cause, the more comprehensive it is, and the further its effects reach." Souls, which are "incorporeal, separable from bodies and indestructible/immortal," represent "the lowest level of entities that are capable of reverting upon itself." Types of souls that participate in this causality loop include divine, demonic, human, and animal. Proclus held, in

---

[1] *Proclus Elemental Theology* 35, in Thomas M. Johnson, trans., *Proclus' Metaphysical Elements* (Osceola, MO, 1909), pp. 31 f., also quoted in part in "Proclus" in *SEP.*
[2] *Elem. Theol.* 28 in Johnson, p. 27; see also "Proclus" in *SEP.*

contradiction to the astronomer Ptolemy, that even the planets possess intelligent souls by which they move.[1]

Theurgic Neoplatonists not only believed that everything is related to everything else, but that "all reality ... is directed upwards towards the origin from which it proceeds," thus forming a "chain." Therefore, "symbols [can] establish the secret correspondences between sensible things (stones, plants, and animals) and celestial and divine realities."[2] Ritual acts and the use of *hieratic* objects "worked because of some occult sympathy between the material elements used and the constitution of the divine."[3] The Theurgists somehow rationalized, as well, that lower orders of beings actually appeal to higher orders of beings, with which they engage in a "sympathetic" relationship,[4] as portrayed in the graphic image below:[5]

```
The One (Unity)   -------------------------
                                           |
Being     ----------------------------     |
                                     |      |
Life      ---------------------      |      |
                               |     |      |
Nous      -----------------    |     |      |
                         |     |     |      |
Soul (Reason) ---------  |     |     |      |
                      |  |     |     |      |
Animals  <---------------     |     |      |
                      |  |     |     |      |
Plants   <----------------------     |      |
                         |            |      |
Inanimate bodies  <------------------      |
                                           |
Hyle (Formless Matter) <-------------------
```

---

[1] "Proclus" in *SEP*.

[2] *Ibid.*

[3] Louth, p. 159.

[4] *Ibid.*, pp. 77, 157.

[5] Graphic text-based image of uncertain authorship but possibly attributable to Gary Zabel of UMass-Boston, found at http://www.faculty.umb.edu/gary_zabel/Courses/Phil 281b/Philosophy of Magic/Arcana/Neoplatonism/Proclus.htm, as well as http://www.kheper.net/topics/Neoplatonism/Proclus-lifeof.html.

Thus Proclus held that a sympathetic bond could exist between an object in the material world and an entity in the higher reality of the *forms*,[1] and priestly acts using select sacramental elements could be used profitably to access and "massage" that relationship.

> The theurgist's aim was, through incantations and the mysterious properties of certain stones, herbs and other material substances, to set in motion a chain of sympathies running up through a whole 'series' to the god he was trying to evoke, and so to produce a divine apparition and attain a sort of magical and external communion with the divine being. The practice of theurgy implied ... that the effects of a higher principle reached further down the scale of being than the effects of a lower principle .... Thus for Proclus matter (and consequently the material objects used by the theurgists) participated in the One through fewer intervening terms than the human soul or intellect; and the most direct way to the divine was consequently through theurgy and not through philosophical speculation. (It would be an interesting and valuable exercise to work out the differences between this conception and Catholic sacramentalism.)[2]

One familiar with sound interpretation of Scripture can see, clearly, how contrary to the New-Testament mode of worship is this concept of spirituality, and how dangerous to Biblical Christianity, especially when applied to mystical prayer and sacramental theology. (For instance, from the concept of a sympathy held by higher entities for material objects one may infer *Sacramental Realism* in terms of a sacrifice or offering that moves the divine to act with spiritual efficacy—as it appears that some theologians have done—in a kind of *quid pro quo*). The modern philosopher Hegel was to observe:

> In Proclus we have the culminating point of the Neo-Platonic philosophy; this method in philosophy is carried into later times, continuing even through the whole of the Middle Ages. .... Although the Neo-Platonic school ceased to exist outwardly, ideas of the Neo-Platonists, and specially the philosophy of Proclus, were long maintained and preserved in the Church .... In the earlier, purer, mystical scholastics we find the same ideas as are

---

[1] Itter, p. 76.

[2] Arthur Hilary Armstrong, *An Introduction to Ancient Philosophy* (London: Methuen & Co., 1947), p. 202.

seen in Proclus, and until comparatively recent times, when in the Catholic Church God is spoken of in a profound and mystical way, the ideas expressed are Neo-Platonic.[1]

Pseudo-Dionysius (Denys) "the Areopagite" (c. 500)

Dionysius, whose true identity is unknown but who wrote pseudony-mously in the name of Paul's convert mentioned in Acts 17:34, is "ball park" dated to about A.D. 500. Scholars have compiled a list of proofs of these assertions, which include the lack of mention of his name or his writings by any of the Church Fathers; his familiarity with Neo-platonism, Theurgy, and the philosophy of Proclus; the influence of Gregory of Nyssa; his mention of singing the creed (an unknown prac-tice before the late Fifth Century); his familiarity with the liturgy and hierarchy of the Eastern Church of the period; a reference to his works by Severus of Antioch in the period A.D. 518 to 528; and a Monophy-site embassy citing one of his works at a conference in A.D. 532.[2]

The anonymity and pseudonymity of Dionysius' writings have caused him to be confused not only with the actual first-century con-vert by that name but with the martyred third-century Bishop of Paris, Denis, who became the patron saint of France. Worse still, this confu-sion has served to grant him "almost apostolic" status and an audience beyond his expectations—a notoriety perpetuated by a document, the Areopagitica, written by Hilduin, Abbot of St. Denis, at the behest of Louis the Pious, and a translation of his works by John Scotus Eriu-gena.[3] Nevertheless, Dionysius' apparent subterfuge is defended in some quarters as an example of *declamatio*, "a long established rhetor-ical device."[4]

Dionysius, whoever he was, made it his business to apply Neopla-tonist and Theurgical principles and methodology to Christian wor-

---

[1] Georg Wilhelm Friedrich Hegel, *Lectures on the History of Philosophy*, vol. 2, trans. E. S. Haldane and Frances H. Simson (London: Kegan Paul, Trench, Trübner & Co., 1894), pp. 450 f., also quoted in part in "Proclus" in *SEP*.
[2] Bigg, p. 340; Louth, pp. 155 f.; John F. Wippel, *Metaphysical Themes in Thomas Aquinas, Studies in Philosophy and the History of Philosophy*, vol. 10 (Wash., D.C.: The Catholic University of America Press, 1984), p. 221; "Pseudo-Dionysius the Areopagite" in *SEP* at http://plato.stanford.edu/entries/pseudo-dionysius-areopagite/.
[3] Bigg, p. 340; "Pseudo" in *SEP*; Mosheim, vol. 2, pp. 331 f.; "St. Denis" in *CE* at http://www.newadvent.org/cathen/04721a.htm.
[4] "Pseudo" in *SEP*.

ship, liturgy, and ecclesiology. He is thought to have been a student of Proclus or of his school.[1] It has been suggested that his immediate teacher was the mentor he calls Hierotheus, probably also a pseudonym.[2] Since his name can be taken to mean, "priest of God," he might simply serve as a metaphor and/or a fiction of convenience. Perhaps Hierotheus or Dionysius, like Justin Martyr, saw himself as a Christian philosopher and established his own since-forgotten school.

(Dionysius may be compared to E. W. Kenyon, who attended Emerson College, known for its study of Metaphysics; who decided to resolve Metaphysics with Christianity, and was followed and even plagiarized by Kenneth Hagin, Sr., resulting in much of the "Word of Faith" doctrine.)[3]

Dionysius perpetuates the Platonic and Neoplatonic ideas that God resides in thick darkness, is unknowable, and cannot be adequately described with human words or categories. He develops the theory that Biblical descriptions of God which appear out of character, such as a man awakened out of sleep or drunken in Psalm 78:65, alert the interpreter to "symbols" which can be "useful for theology"[4] but cannot be taken literally or merely figuratively.

Instead of simply feeling free to apply allegorical interpretation (like Origen) by this lack of understanding, these are to him "dissimilar similarities" that are unintelligible and therefore must be understood as hidden symbols or metaphors in order to become intelligible. The metaphor of God as a drunken warrior becomes to him a picture of "the overloaded measurelessness of all goods in the one who is their cause." By this approach, the "name" or description of God becomes to the interpreter a new source of "intelligible truth." These understandings cannot be derived intellectually through study or thought but must be revealed as a spiritual gift. While Dionysius gives "lip service" to revealed Scripture as the source of this truth, he demonstrates a reliance on "special revelation" as well as extrabiblical sources.[5]

---

[1] *Ibid.*

[2] *Ibid.*; Bigg. p. 341.

[3] See D. R. McConnell, *A Different Gospel* (Peabody, MA: Hendrickson, 1988).

[4] "Pseudo" in *SEP.*

[5] *Ibid.*

Like Philo, Origen, and Gregory of Nyssa, Dionysius cites the example of Moses' glimpse of God. Moses undergoes an *ascent* toward God, for which he must first acquire purificatory virtues, for God is "manifested without veil and in truth" to those who pass through contemplation and theology and "alone who pass through both all things consecrated and pure, and ascend above every ascent of all holy summits, and leave behind all divine lights and sounds, and heavenly words, and enter into the gloom, where really is, as the Oracles say, He Who is beyond all."[1] However, "even then he does not meet with Almighty God Himself, but views not Him (for He is viewless) but the place where He is," for God is unknowable and in darkness. Yet, approaching God, "he (Moses) is freed from them who are both seen and seeing, and enters into the gloom of the *Agnosia* ["Unknowing"]; a gloom veritably mystic, within which he closes all perceptions of knowledge and enters into the altogether impalpable and unseen, being wholly of Him Who is beyond all, and of none, neither himself nor other; and by inactivity of all knowledge, united in his better part to the altogether Unknown, and by knowing nothing, knowing above mind."[2] Thus Moses achieves *Mystical Union* (*henosis*) with God, where spiritual formation can occur—a theology by which Dionysius reveals his dependence on Plotinus as well as Philo.

Knowing a selection of "divine names" with which to approach God is vital to Dionysius. It is only after thorough contemplation of divine names that one can advance to silence, darkness, "unknowing," and can then experience Unity.[3] This *ascent* presumably takes place not in private devotions, for the most part, but in the worship of the church. Dionysius describes nine types of angels, in groups of three (a "triad of triads"), and likewise a hierarchy of three threes in the church. The highest triad in the ecclesiastical (church) hierarchy is made up of rites or sacraments: the Oil of Anointing, the Eucharist, and Water Baptism; the second consists of bishops (*hierarchs*), priests (*hiereis*), and

---

[1] *Mystic Theology* 1.3 in John Parker, *The Works of Dionysius the Areopagite*, vol. 1 (London: James Parker and Co., 1897), pp. 131 f.; also mentioned in "Pseudo" in *SEP*.
[2] Parker, p. 132.
[3] "Pseudo" in *SEP*.

deacons (*leitourgoi*, "liturgists"); followed by monks, the baptized, and a mixed group of catechumens, penitents, and the demon-possessed.[1]

Through the rites of the Church, only the *hierarchs* (or perhaps the entire rank of three constituted by ministers) may contemplate, directly, the intelligible realm (of *forms*, one presumes)—the realm visible and accessible to the angels. The *hierarchs* perform their rites not for themselves but for the benefit of the lower ranks, who can only perceive the "visible realm," thus requiring visible symbols to activate their contemplation. These "symbols" are made up of both physical acts (rituals) and objects, including bread, wine, anointing oil, and (one may surmise) also holy water. Within the context of the liturgical worship these sacramental objects acquire spiritual efficacy, and rites "clothe themselves in words."[2] This construct provides philosophical support for *Sacerdotalism* and establishes a functional "chain" of "go-betweens" necessary for common people to reach God.

As in Proclus, everything is related to everything else. Spiritually speaking, the hierarchies represent a chain of "vertical connected-ness,"[3] and the system of rites and incantations (liturgy) and use of symbols (objects, sacraments) reflects Proclus' conception of *cause and effect*, such that each visible *effect* (as in the partaking of wine) relates to—has sympathy toward—its *cause* (as in Christ's sacrifice). In return, these objects attract a natural *receptivity* (*epitedeiotes*)[4] from their *cause* (source, *form*), resulting in spiritual efficacy. Water Baptism, the Eucharisf, and Anointing thus become, spiritually, "replica-tions" of the works of God they symbolize,[5] an idea which suggests the theological errors of *Baptismal Regeneration*, *Sacramental Realism*, and *Apostolic Succession*, respectively.

---

[1] Louth, pp. 163 f.; contrast "Pseudo" in *SEP*.
[2] "Pseudo" in *SEP*.
[3] *Ibid.*
[4] Itter, p. 76.
[5] *Ibid.*, p. 80.

Chapter 7. The Continuing Influence of Paganized Christianity

In the future, the present writer might choose to trace the influences of Pagan theology more extensively, and in detail, down to the present day. Additional avenues of pertinent study would be an examination of the psychology behind Mysticism (what inner needs and desires compel practitioners to crave and seek mystical experience, according to the testimony of expert sources, and why Mystics so intractably defend their practice in spite of its contradictions of Scripture) as well as the politics behind the sacramental/sacerdotal system.

For now, it is appropriate to close the present study with a selection of examples of the later effects of the injection of Pagan philosophy into Christian theology.

John Scotus Eriugena (c. 810–c. 877)

As mentioned earlier, Eriugena (or Erigena) translated the works attributed to Pseudo-Dionysius, long popular in the East, into Latin, which made them available to the Western Church. He likewise translated and propagated works by Gregory of Nyssa and Maximus the Confessor.[1] Eriugena "made it his aim to elucidate the vague theories of Dionysius, and to present them as a consistent philosophical system worked out by the help of Aristotle and perhaps Boethius." This fueled an exercise in speculation which Inge, himself a Neoplatonist, labels "audacious."[2] Eriugena thereafter gives rein to the "most dangerous tendencies" of Dionysius as well as Origen and the Alexandrian Fathers.[3]

In his time, Eriugena enjoyed the patronage and protection of Charles the Bald. Over the ensuing centuries, many of his works were

---

[1] "John Scottus Eriugena" in *SEP* at http://plato.Stanford.edu/entries/scottus-eriugena/.
[2] William Ralph Inge, *Christian Mysticism* (NY: Charles Scribner's Sons, 1899), p. 133; see also Mosheim, vol. 2, p. 332.
[3] Inge, *CM*, p. 137.

condemned by bishops' councils, yet he maintained a strong following, including Hugh of St. Victor, Meister Eckhart, and Nicholas of
Cusa; and in the 19th Century, Hegelians.[1]

Bonaventure (1221–1274)

The Franciscans were founded by Francis of Assisi in 1209.
Their leader in the middle of the century was Bonaventure, a
traditionalist who defended the theology of Augustine and the
philosophy of Plato, incorporating only a little of Aristotle in with
the more neoplatonist elements. Following Anselm, Bonaventure
supposed that reason can only discover truth when philosophy is
illuminated by religious faith.[2]

Thomas Aquinas (1225–1274)

The textbooks credit Aquinas with being an Aristotelian, rationalist
scholastic, yet Inge calls him "nearer to Plotinus than to the real Aristotle."[3]   John F. Wippel[4] catalogs a number of instances in which
Aquinas's theology follows Plato (pp. 287, 288), Dionysius (pp. 9,
144, 159, 164, 287, 288), or some other Neoplatonist (pp. 10, 281), as
well as Augustine's *Book of Eighty-Three Questions* (pp. 287 f.),
rather than Aristotle. Dionysius' book on divine names was one of
Aquinas's favorites, though in some ways misapprehended.[5]

Aquinas outlines three ways in which God can be known: reason,
revelation, and intuition,[6] the nature of which he does not fully
explain, but is comparable to the three "stages" of Gregory of Nyssa,
and bears every appearance of a neat Neoplatonic *triad*.

Following the teaching of Dionysius, "names of pure perfections do
signify the divine substance albeit in deficient and imperfect fashion.
Since every agent [cause, *form*] acts insofar as it is in act (*sic.*), and
therefore produces something like itself [*i.e.*, effect, shadow], the form

---

[1] "Eriugena" in *SEP*.
[2] "Scholasticism" at http://en.wikipedia.org/wiki/Scholasticism).
[3] Russell, p. 284.
[4] John F. Wippel, *Metaphysical Themes in Thomas Aquinas II, in Studies in
Philosophy and the History of Philosophy*, vol. 47 (The Catholic University of
America Press, 2007).
[5] Louth, p. 155.
[6] Russell, p. 460.

of any effect must be present in its efficient cause in some way,"[1] which goes right back to the Proclian/Dionysian concept of names as symbols having *sympathy* toward their originating *forms*, *i.e.*, *effects* that appeal to their *receptive causes*.

A divine idea, according to Aquinas, "exists in God"; moreover, following Aristotle, "like produces like."[2]   "The sacramental event"— now following Neoplatonism—has a "single hidden origin in the 'being, living and thinking' of contingent beings"; therefore "sacraments function as events which bring believers into harmony with this origin."[3]   In this "context, sacramental grace is defined according to a causality-scheme" in such a way that it "causes/realises what it signifies," which is grace "produced" by God.[4] Since "grace is nothing else than a certain shared similitude to the divine nature" (Aquinas), following the circular reasoning that sacraments are the "means of grace" that God has provided, then it is the sacraments by which "God produces grace."[5]

Today, this Dionysian subtext, bequeathed through Aquinas, is reflected with remarkable exactitude in modern expressions of Catholic doctrine:

> According to Catholic theology, a dynamic link exists between these sacramental signs and the realities they signify. The outward sign is not just a symbol of divine grace, rather sacraments are efficacious signs: they do not merely represent a sacred reality but themselves cause the reality they represent. …. Accordingly, the outward signs of the sacraments are dynamic signs and instruments of grace, visible and tangible realities dignified through their involvement in the sanctification of humanity.[6]

Besides sacramental grace, Aquinas presents a mode, if not a methodology, by which a soul may transcend, albeit temporarily, to *Mysti-*

---

[1] Wippel, p. 159.

[2] *Ibid.*, p. 164.

[3] Boeve, p. 7.

[4] *Ibid.*

[5] *Ibid.*, pp. 7-8.

[6] Helena M. Tomko, "Introduction: Sacramental Realism," in *Sacramental Realism: Gertrud von le Fort and German Catholic Literature in the Weimar Republic and Third Reich (1924-46)*, MHRA Texts and Dissertations, vol. 68, Bithell Series of Dissertations, vol. 31 (Leeds, UK: Maney Publishing, 2007), p. 2.

cal Union with God. The only means he admits is "by grace," through having been granted the *lumen gloriae*, the "light of glory." This "vision of God by the blessed in Heaven is not mere vision, but union," writes A. B. Sharpe. It does not come by a Plotinian "discursive intellectual process"; rather, "they see God as He is in Himself, not from a distance ... but from within."[1] This degree of personal revelation of God, one notes, is certainly a bold claim, if not to say a presumption, one hardly made by the Prophets. The picture of transcendence which Aquinas presents perhaps describes ecstasy, of the Augustinian type, but goes beyond ecstasy. It does not seem to go quite so far as "displacement" or "possession" as Philo ascribed to the Prophets, since "self-consciousness" remains; but seems definitely to describe a *superimposition* of God's mind on one's own,[2] which one presumes automatically produces *spiritual formation—apotheosis*, if not *theopoiesis*.

The experience of the *lumen gloriae* may presumably be equated with the "changeless light" of Augustine, and the illuminations described in the experiences of John of the Cross and Teresa of Avila.[3] John's concept of "the dark night of the soul" was strongly influenced by Dionysius, whom he often quotes, as well as by Gregory of Nyssa.[4]

> The celestial hierarchy of Dionysius and the benign daemons of Proclus, the powers invoked by Pagan or by Christian theurgy, by Platonist, by Cabbalist, or by saint, alike reward the successful aspirant with supernatural endowments; and so far Apollonius of Tyana and Peter of Alcantara, Asclepigenia and St. Theresa, must occupy as religious magicians the same province. The error is in either case the same—a divine efficacy is attributed to rites and formulas, sprinklings or fumigations, relics or incantations, of mortal manufacture.[5]

Interestingly, John himself warns at some length of the risk of mistaking natural phenomena and experiences of specious origin for the

---

[1] Alfred Bowyer Sharpe, *Mysticism: Its True Nature and Value*, 2nd ed. (London: Sands & Company, 1910), pp. 93, 95.

[2] See *Ibid.*, pp. 93 f.

[3] *Ibid.*, pp. 99 f.

[4] Louth, p. 176.

[5] Vaughan, p. 46.

revelation of God.[1] Neither John nor Teresa "address themselves to any consideration of the mode, whether partially natural or wholly supernatural, in which the supernatural effects are produced."[2]

Dante Alighieri (c. 1265–1321)

Dante writes in *Paradiso* 28:127-135:

> Those orders upwards all intensely gaze,
> And prevail below, that towards God
> All are attracted, whilst they all attract.
> And with such mighty longings Denys sought
> To contemplate those Orders, that he names,
> And, like myself, described them in detail.
> But Gregory thought not afterwards as he;
> Whence and so soon as in this heaven his eyes
> Were opened, he at his own error smiled.[3]

Dante's divine hierarchy, then, was based on that of Pseudo-Dionysius, whom he seems to regard as a prophet. Pope Gregory the Great, who disagreed somewhat with Dionysius, and with whom Dante had some differences, is seen acknowledging his errors with a smile.

E. R. Dodds points back even further to Plotinus as the theological source and watershed in Christian thinking: "In [*The Enneads*] converge almost all the main currents of thought that come down from eight hundred years of Greek speculation; out of it there issues a new current, destined to fertilize minds as different as those of Augustine and Boethius, Dante and Meister Eckhart, Coleridge, Bergson and Mr. T. S. Eliot."[4]

John Wesley (1703–1791)

Advocates and defenders of John Wesley are quick to assert that any elements of Neoplatonism and Mysticism within the order of the An-

---

[1] Sharpe, p. 102.

[2] *Ibid.*, pp. 108 f.

[3] David Johnston, trans., *A Translation of Dante's Paradiso* (Bath, UK: Printed at the Chronicle Office, 1868), p. 171, also quoted in part by Louth, p. 155.

[4] E. R. Dodds, "Tradition and Personal Achievement in the Philosophy of Plotinus," *The Journal of Roman Studies*, vol. 50/1-2 (1960), p. 1; also quoted in part from another source by Louth, p. 35.

glican Church were well-known and acknowledged, suitably dealt-with, and adequately mitigated. It is moreover suggested that Wesley, if accused of harboring any such influences, hardly introduced them himself. John Cassian, as mentioned in Chapter 6, had introduced Evagrius to the Western Church, and "had physically brought back with him Basil's Institutes, a work which would serve as a model for western monastic rules, including Benedict's." These ideas signify-cantly influenced Thomas á Kempis and later mystics, including the Jansenists and Port-Royalists, "their Augustinian orientation notwith-standing."[1]

By the Seventeenth Century, English intellectuals and divines had rediscovered many works of the Eastern Mystics, and began to publish new editions. The "Cambridge Platonists," in particular, turned away from Aristotle and Scholasticism and renewed interest in Plato.[2] An-glicanism, seeking a "middle way" (*via media*) of compromise be-tween salvation by faith alone and salvation by works, found especially in the works of John Chrysostom a "forgotten strand of *theosis*," as Steve McCormick describes it, in the guise of "divine-human participation."[3]   But then, Thomas Cranmer, in the time of Henry VIII, had already incorporated Neoplatonic "participation" into the *Book of Common Prayer*, namely, his homilies "Of Salvation," "Of the True, Lively and Christian Faith," and "Of Good Works Annexed Unto Faith." Together, these comprise the formal expression of Angli-can *soteriology*.[4]   In 1738, John Wesley abridged Cranmer's three homilies into "his first doctrinal manifesto."[5]

The son of an Anglican *rector* (local priest), Wesley was steeped in Anglicanism, which he never abandoned. His father, Samuel, parti-cularly enamored of Chrysostom, urged his son to obtain a copy of

---

[1] David Bundy, "Christian Virtue: John Wesley and the Alexandrian Tradition," *Wesleyan Theological Journal* 26 (1991):142.

[2] Mark Goldie, 'Cambridge Platonists (act. 1630s–1680s),' *Oxford Dictionary of National Biography*, Oxford University Press, Sept 2013 (http://www.oxforddnb.-com/view/theme/94274, accessed March 27, 2014). The Cambridge Platonists might have had fairly direct influence on John Wesley through his father, whose friend was John Norris, see Bundy, p. 142.

[3] K. Steve McCormick, "Theosis in Chrysostom and Wesley: An Eastern Paradigm on Faith and Love," *Wesleyan Theological Journal* 26 (1991):49-50.

[4] *Ibid.*, p. 66, see also 67.

[5] *Ibid.*, p. 67.

Chrysostom's work, *On the Priesthood* (*De sacerdotia*), with the words, "Master it: digest it"; and later, "Master St. Chrysostom, our Articles and the form of Ordination." "If I were to preach in Greek," Samuel wrote, "St. Chrysostom should be my master."[1] John was further encouraged to study the Church Fathers, especially those of the first three centuries of the Christian era, by John Clayton, an accomplished Patristics scholar.[2]

> Wesley learned from his father to appreciate the ancient pastoral theologians: Chrysostom, Basil, Athanasius and Cyprian (*Advice to a Young Clergyman*).[3]

Wesley later recommended the Eastern Fathers, and borrowed heavily from Chrysostom in his own *Address to Clergy* (1756).[4] He wrote, for instance,

> Can any who spend several years in those seats of learning, be excused, if they do not add to that of the languages and sciences, the knowledge of the Fathers? The most authentic commentators on Scripture, as being both nearest the fountain, and eminently endued with that Spirit by whom "all Scripture was given?" It will be easily perceived, I speak chiefly of those who wrote before the Council of Nice[a]. But who would not likewise desire to have some acquaintance with those that followed them? With St. Chrysostom, Basil, Jerome, [Augustine]; and above all, that man of a broken heart, Ephraim Syrus?[5]

In his writings and preaching, Wesley "Frequently cited ... Basil, Chrysostom, Clement of Alexandria, Clement of Rome, Ephraem Syrus, Ignatius, Irenaeus, Justin Martyr, Origen, Polycarp and (Pseudo-)Macarius." The latter, Pseudo-Macarius, was to become a significant influence on Wesley's doctrines: in particular, those of "Prevenient Grace" and "Christian Perfection." While Wesley at times

---

[1] *Ibid.*, p. 50.

[2] Albert C. Outler, ed., *John Wesley* (NY: Oxford University Press, 1964; paperback, 1980), p. 9, and Michael J. Christensen, "Theosis and Sanctification: John Wesley's Reformulation of a Patristic Doctrine," *Wesleyan Theological Journal* 31/2 (Fall 1996):75.

[3] Christensen, p. 75.

[4] McCormick, p. 50, Christensen, p. 74.

[5] John Wesley, *The Miscellaneous Works of the Rev. John Wesley* (NY: J. & J. Harper, 1828), p. 70, also quoted from another source in McCormick, pp. 50-51.

differs with Macarius in details, clearly "the similarities are much stronger than the differences ...."[1]

Wesley himself described several of the other early influences on his devotional life as well as his theology:

> In the year 1725, being in the twenty-third year of my age, I met with Bishop Taylor's *Rules and Exercises of Holy Living and Dying*. In reading several parts of this book, I was exceedingly affected with that part in particular which relates to purity of intention....
>
> In the year 1726, I met with Kempis's 'Christian Pattern.' The nature and extent of inward religion, the religion of the heart, now appeared to me in a stronger light than ever it had done before. I saw, that giving even all my life to God, (supposing it possible to do this and go no farther,) would profit me nothing, unless I gave my heart, yea, all my heart, to him. I saw that 'simplicity of intention and purity of affection,' one design in all we speak or do, and one desire, ruling all our tempers, are indeed 'the wings of the soul,' without which she can never ascend to the mount of God.
>
> A year or two after, Mr. Law's 'Christian Perfection,' and 'Serious Call,' were put into my hands. These convinced me, more than ever, of the absolute impossibility of being half a Christian.[2]

Over the course of his life, Wesley utilized a great many recent secondary works that applied Eastern principles, and (as we shall see) created others of his own. Kempis he found too pessimistic: "I cannot think, that when God sent us into the world, he had irreversibly decreed, that we should be perpetually miserable in it,"[3] yet Wesley largely embraced his concepts of self-abnegation and *ascent*. William

---

[1] Randy L. Maddox, "John Wesley and Eastern Orthodoxy: Influences, Convergences, and Differences," *Asbury Theological Journal* 45/2 (1990):30, 31, 35; see also Outler, pp. 9-10, and Christensen, p. 74.

[2] Henry Moore, *The Life of the Rev. John Wesley, A. M.*, vol. I (London: Printed for John Kershaw, 1824), p. 161. Regarding "purity of intention," Runyon writes, "If the intention is right, this is what really counts [to Wesley]. 'Intention' was a theme important to him from his 1725 self-dedication onward," Theodore Runyon, "The New Creation: A Wesleyan Distinctive," *Wesleyan Theological Journal* 31/2 (Fall 1996):12.

[3] Moore., p. 124.

Law had been a mentor to John and his brother Charles.[1] Law and Jeremy Taylor were both attempting to construct "patristic primitivist syntheses of the virtuous Christian life, viewing it developmentally."[2] Law had visited the Wesley home on many occasions and had a profound effect on the siblings, such that Charles Wesley suggested much later, "Mr. Law was our John the Baptist."[3] Law was one of the select individuals that John Wesley consulted before committing to his Georgia mission.[4]

Wesley's enthusiasm for William Beveridge further exposed him to Chrysostom, the two combining to serve as the apparent origin of his conception of restoring the image of God (ultimately Platonic) by virtue of the "energy of love."

> Wesley found this notion, which is, again, the eastern idea of *theosis*, of divine-human participation, a characteristic note in the homilies of Chrysostom, and in the liturgy, the homilies, and the Thirty-nine Articles of Religion of the Church of England. Wesley was to take that motif of divine-human participation in the *via salutis* and weave it throughout his *ordo salutis* [*i.e.*, integrate a Neoplatonic "way of salvation" into his conception of the "order of salvation"].[5]

Sailing for Georgia aboard the *Simmonds*, 1735, Wesley busied himself studying the German language, along with devotional reading and his accustomed Christian disciplines. He had managed to procure a library of over sixty volumes, many of them of recent Anglican authorship, but also including Beveridge's *Pandectae*, William Cave's *Primitive Christianity*, and a large assortment of Eastern liturgical works.[6] It was probably Cave's book that introduced him to Pseudo-Macarius and Ephraim of Syria. Thus Wesley absorbed Neoplatonic ideas "about the stages of divine ascent, holiness of heart, progressive perfection, and the affective manifestations of the Holy Spirit in the life of the believer."[7]

---

[1] Christensen, p. 75.

[2] Bundy, p. 141.

[3] Moore, p. 107.

[4] *Ibid.*, p. 234, see also 190.

[5] *Ibid.*, p. 54.

[6] Outler, p. 12, Christensen, p. 75.

[7] Christensen, pp. 76, 85.

During a particularly severe storm at sea, he was highly impressed by the calmness displayed by the Moravians on board. He had already studied the mystic work, *Theologica Germanica.*[1] Arriving in Georgia, he was similarly impressed by Rev. Spangenberg, of Savannah, but hedged when the Moravian asked him, "Does the Spirit of God bear witness with your spirit that you are a child of God?" to which Wesley weakly replied, "I know He is the Saviour of the world," and "I hope He has died to save me."[2] In spite of his Christian disciplines, Wesley had been all full of doubts all through the voyage. Later still, he wrote in his journal,

> It is now two years and almost four months since I left my native country in order to teach the Georgian Indians the nature of Christianity. But what have I learned myself in the meantime? Why (what I the least of all suspected), that I, who went to America to convert others, was never myself converted to God.[3]

During the subsequent debacle in Georgia, Wesley obtained a Moravian hymnal, and spent three to five hours a day translating and adapting, in all, thirty-three German hymns, according to his own purposes and inclinations. Among these was the Gerhard Tersteegen hymn, rendered in English, "Thou Hidden Love of God, Whose Height," one of four by Tersteegen that he translated, and the one most often published thereafter in English hymnals.[4] One commentator suggests that "this hymn might be seen as one of the clearest reflections of Wesley's own spiritual yearning...."[5] (Yearning appears to be a common indicator of mystic propensities and appeal.) Meanwhile, Wesley also took the opportunity to experiment with new forms of liturgy, which confused and offended his congregation. A local magistrate scolded, "The people ... say *they* are Protestants. But as for *you*, they cannot tell what religion you are of."[6]

---

[1] Moore, p. 190, Bundy, p. 142.

[2] From Chapter 6 of John Telford, *The Life of John Wesley* (http://Wesley.nnu-edu/?id=88, accessed April 2, 2014). This passage is apparently taken from a printing other than that of 1900, in which this and some other passages do not appear.

[3] *Ibid.*, see also McCormick, p. 48.

[4] J. Steven O'Malley, "Pietistic Influence on John Wesley: Wesley and Gerhard Tersteegen" *Wesleyan Theological Journal* 31/2 (Fall 1996):49, 65, 66.

[5] O'Malley, p. 57 f.

[6] Outler, pp. 12-13, see also Bundy, p. 141.

The Methodist mission to Georgia was a fiasco. Charles proved a maladroit secretary to General Oglethorpe; John, a tactless pastor, Ingham and Delamotte, ineffectual assistants.[1]

In 1738, abandoning Georgia under a cloud, Wesley returned to England, where he and Charles almost immediately became involved with the Fetter Lane Moravian group. That May, he had an emotional experience that he counted as his belated conversion, and by September, he was off to visit the German Pietists at Herrnhut.

> The representatives of this tradition who influenced Wesley began with the Dominican mysticism of Johann Tauler (1300-1361), and proceeded to the distinctive Reformed spirituality of Gerhard Tersteegen (1697-1769)."[2]

Always seeking his own "assurance of faith," Wesley asked one Arvid Gradin to provide, in writing, his definition of the concept. Gradin's reply concluded with, "a deliverance from every fleshly desire, and a cessation of all, even inward sins"—it would seem, as it did to Wesley, a confirmation of his own developing view of Perfection.[3] "Spiritually bankrupt, without peace and joy or the assurance of salvation, he embraced the Moravian approach to 'faith alone' and 'full salvation.'"[4] On the negative side, Wesley found Herrnhut to be in the midst of controversy with the brethren at Halle. The Hallensians regarded the necessity of an extended "penitential struggle" (*Bußkampf*) leading eventually to a "breakthrough" (*Durchbruch*) to gain assurance of saving faith, whereas the Herrnhuters had gravitated toward a quick and easy, "affective" acceptance.[5] Wesley soon became disenchanted with their polemics and with Count von Zinzendorf, thereafter distancing himself from the Moravians.[6] "The English writers," he wrote, "such as Bishop Beveridge, Bishop Taylor, and Mr. Nelson, a little relieved me from these well-meaning, wrong-headed Germans."[7] Yet

---

[1] *Ibid.*, p. 11.
[2] O'Malley, p. 49.
[3] John Wesley, *A Plain Account of Christian Perfection*, in Wesley and Fletcher, *Entire Sanctification Attainable in This Life* (London: Charles H. Kelly, 1898), p. 11.
[4] Christensen, p. 76.
[5] O'Malley, p. 51.
[6] Tersteegen had previously questioned von Zinzendorf's self-interest and possible antinomianism, O'Malley, p. 57.
[7] Moore, p. 343.

he continued to value many of the German Pietist hymns, especially those of Tersteegen.[1]

Through Wesley, it has been said, Tersteegen's spirituality has reached millions of English-speaking people. John Nuelson, a German Methodist, granted that Wesley's dissemination of German hymns had strongly influenced the Methodists' doctrine of Perfection. With Tersteegen's ideas came the influence of French Quietists, English Philadelphians, and Berleburg Bible Pietists, along with all the Patristic, mystical, and ascetic works that Tersteegen had translated and edited. He spoke in terms of a *Seelengrund* (a term garnered from Eckhart and Tauler), an "inward soul" capable of longing for God. This inward soul may possess an "inward inclination" (*Grundneigung*) able to respond to the "wooing" of Christ's Prevenient Grace (as Wesley would perceive it), such that it "makes room" (*Raum gebe*) for God's presence. From that *Seelengrund*, Christ purposes "to expand His gracious influence to encompass the cognitive, volitional, affective, and relational aspects of one's existence,"[2] in other words, *spiritual formation*. Yet Tersteegen, in spite of other Plotinian affinities, discouraged seekers from *introspection*, that being idolatry; rather to "turn your inward eye from yourself," fixing one's gaze on Christ.[3] He considered the imputation of righteousness to be instantaneous, but the transformation to Christ-likeness to be progressive (*contra* Wesley), the goal being to renew in believers the image of Christ (so also Wesley).[4]

Besides Tersteegen, Pseudo-Macarius and Ephraim of Syria were particular favorites of Wesley, from whom he sought devotional material and theological fodder, mining for ideas and modes of expression. Besides his aforementioned contribution to Prevenient Grace, Macarius further contributed to Wesley's *soteriology* (as had Tersteegen)— one point of difference being "that Wesley understood perfection primarily as an identifiable, instantaneously-achieved state, while Macarius emphasized the tenacious entrenchment of sin in even the most

---

[1] O'Malley, p. 53, see also 57.

[2] *Ibid.*, pp. 49, 57-61.

[3] *Ibid.*, p. 69, incl. note 77, referring to L. G. Harvey, ed., *Tersteegen, Recluse in Demand: Life and Letters*, vol. I (Hampton, TN: Harvey & Tait, n.d.), pp. 125, 129.

[4] *Ibid.*, p. 65; see also Bundy, p. 153, and Christensen, p. 71, note 1.

mature Christian and the constant need to seek God through prayer."[1] "This great gift of God," Wesley wrote, "the salvation of our souls, is no other than the image of God fresh stamped on our hearts. It is a 'renewal of believers in the spirit of their minds, after the likeness of Him that created them.'"[2] Certainly Wesley's views on grace appear to be more closely derived from Macarius and Eastern theology in general than from, as one might expect, Arminius.[3] Wesley, one will note, believed that the *Fifty Spiritual Homilies* were the work of "Macarius of Egypt," a fourth-century Desert Father, rather than a pseudonymous writer now widely purported to have been a fifth-century Syrian monk, strongly influenced by Gregory of Nyssa.[4]

Wesley's exposure to Ephraim of Syria, whom he called "the man of the broken heart," goes back to his Holy Club days at Oxford. Ephraim taught self-abnegation, contemplation, *theosis*, and an ante-Nicene view of man yearning to return to an "angelic" original state. Michael Christensen and Randy Maddox suggest that Ephraim's "luminous eye" figure "is similar to if not the source of Wesley's doctrine of 'spiritual senses'" (a concept to which Tersteegen probably also contributed, see above). "Spiritual senses," to Wesley, include the faculty of perceiving assurance, both of salvation and Perfection.[5]

Wesley, it is noted, mitigated the *theosis* of Macarius and Ephraim, emphasizing a divine work of grace through love that he posited in the negation of the power of sin and perfection of human *intent*. When Wesley edited the *Homilies* of Macarius for his *Christian Library* series, he excised references to *theosis* as well as *asceticism*.[6]

In regard to Perfection, Wesley expressed concern to his brother Charles that the latter, by aiming at *theosis*, was setting the bar of holiness too high to be realistically attainable.[7] Wesley, says McCormick, had gradually come to understand *soteriology* in the anthropological terms of a "Biblical *eudaemonism*," by which man seeks holiness

---

[1] Maddox, p. 31; on Tersteegen, see also O'Malley, p. 65.

[2] Wesley, *A Plain Account*, p. 25.

[3] So Maddox, pp. 31, 35.

[4] See Christensen, p. 85; Outler, p. 9, note 26; and a somewhat contrary view in Bundy, p. 139.

[5] Christensen, pp. 81, 85, incl. note 19.

[6] See Christensen, pp. 76; 85, note 22; and p. 87. For more on the awakening of spiritual senses, in the views of both Macarius and Wesley, see Runyon, p. 14.

[7] Letter from John to Charles Wesley, June 27, 1766, cited in Christensen, p. 90.

because in holiness man is most happy.[1] Albert Outler suggests that Wesley repositioned the "ladder" of Perfection, after his own scheme, toward becoming "like" God, but short of *becoming* a god.[2] This effectively "domesticated" or even "democratized" the (Plotinian) *ascent* that Eastern Mystics had taught, making "perfection" an "attainable goal."[3] In Wesley's defense, David Bundy insists that he "took much of the [Anglican] synthesis [of Eastern theology] out of the academy, church and cloister and brought it to the people" and "adapted that synthesis in structures of discipline and accountability for laity; and who modeled what he preached."[4] It was "Methodists in America," Outler asserts, who "contributed to a very considerable confusion by interpreting 'perfection' in terms of 'the second blessing' or 'entire sanctification as a state of grace distinct from justification, attainable instantaneously by faith.'"[5]

Wesley's writings reflect many more Eastern Mystic influences besides these three. It is widely recognized (not without considerable dispute, in regard to extent as well as provenance), that Wesley based his tract, *The Character of a Methodist*, and also a published poem, "On Clemens Alexandrinus's Description of a Perfect Christian" on Clement's picture of the "Perfect Gnostic" (from *Stromateis*, Book 7, see also Chapter 6 of this book). Bundy suggests that Wesley might have been exposed to Clement's ideas secondarily through publishing a certain book by Anthony Horneck, and that the poem might rather be attributable to John Gambold.[6] But in a letter to *Lloyd's Evening Post*, Wesley himself stated, "Five or six and thirty years ago, I much admired the character of a perfect Christian drawn up by Clemens Alexandrinus. Five or six and twenty years ago, a thought came to my mind, of drawing such a character myself, only in a more scriptural manner, and mostly in the very words of Scripture ...."[7] Similarly, Wesley "plagiarized" (Bundy's word) John Williams' book, *A Cate-*

---

[1] McCormick, p. 53. "God is the joy of his heart, and the desire of his soul, which is continually crying, 'Whom have I in heaven but Thee'? He is therefore happy in God; yea, always happy...," Wesley, *A Plain Account*, p. 13, see also p. 8.
[2] Outler, p. 31.
[3] Christensen, p. 88, see also p. 80.
[4] Bundy, p. 155.
[5] Outler, p. 30.
[6] Maddox, p. 30; Christensen, pp. 76, 78; Bundy, pp. 139 ff., 149.
[7] Bundy, pp.139, 143, 151.

chism Truly Representing the Doctrines and Practices of the Church of Rome, with an Answer Thereto, in his work of similar title, and Beveridge's *Sunodikon, sive Pandectae Canonum 55. Apostolorum et Conciliorum Ecclesia Graeca Receptorum* "provided grist" for Wesley's "mill."[1]   In fact, the extent of Wesley's interest in affective Eastern spirituality is demonstrable from many of the books he chose to "extract and abridge" in his fifty-volume *A Christian Library* collection, first published in 1750.[2]

Disenchanted with the German Mystics, wary of *asceticism* and *apathy*, doubtful of the possibility of *theosis*, he nevertheless mined them for useful ideas yet shied away from unqualified endorsement.   In time, Wesley even broke with his past mentor William Law.[3]   Around 1734, Law had become an admirer of self-taught Theosophist and Mystic Jakob Böhme, who laid claim to a series of visions.   In his evolving circumspection, Wesley seems to follow once again the example of Tersteegen, who turned away, even within his own circles, from potential antinomianism and the "excessive ecstasy that he perceived could degenerate into idolatrous self-edification or even demonic torment."[4]   Wesley, however, "nonetheless remained in dialogue with these early mentors, edited and 'corrected' them, and recommended them throughout his life."[5]

The results of this "programmatic"[6] selectivity appears to reveal a considered determination *not* to publish, for the most part, primary works by Eastern Mystics.   Primary works are largely absent within the corpus, for which were substituted secondary works of modern provenance.   "Wesley preferred to edit and present the works of the [Anglican] and continental interpreters of the ancient texts rather than to edit and present the ancient texts themselves!" admits Bundy.[7]   Further, Wesley "reconstructed" mystical works, says Christensen, by replacing implications of *theosis* in Eastern theology with his own

---

[1] Bundy, p. 141.
[2] "A Christian Library by John Wesley," *Wesley Center Online* (http://wesley.nnu.edu/john-wesley/a-christian-library/, accessed April 3, 2014).
[3] Christensen, p. 75, Runyon, p. 13, Moore, p. 518.
[4] O'Malley, p. 56 f.
[5] Christensen, p. 76.
[6] Christensen's term, pp. 74, 80.
[7] Bundy, p. 143, see also 142.

formulation and conception of Perfection, or effectively hiding it.[1] For example, when he published twenty-two of Macarius' *Spiritual Homilies* in *A Christian Library*, "Wesley consistently omitted references to ascetic life and to the notion of theosis...."[2] As Frank Baker describes his *modus operandi*, Wesley's editing "mainly involved choice, striking his pen through passages in printed works, changing the words and phrases, and supplying written links from time to time."

> After considerable hesitation he resolved to leave his human sources uncited, 'that nothing might divert the mind of the reader' from the brief notes themselves. He omitted without comment statements with which he did not agree. All his quotations and allusions, however, rephrased as they were in simpler language, honestly sought to represent the essence of his sources.[3]

The extent of Wesley's editing and *revisionism* of such works (for less it cannot justly be called), is clearly demonstrated in the following passage from Macarius that diametrically contradicts Wesley's doctrine of attainable Perfection:

> So this man confesses that he is not perfect or altogether free from sin. He says that the middle wall of partition has been broken through and shattered, and yet, at some point not wholly broken, nor at all times. There are moments when grace kindles up and comforts and refreshes more fully; there are moments when it retreats and clouds over, according as grace itself manages for the man's advantage. But who is there that has come to the perfect measure at particular seasons, and has tasted and had direct experience of that world? A perfect Christian man, one completely free, I have not yet seen. Although one and another is at rest in grace, and enters into mysteries and revelations and into much sweetness of grace, still sin is yet present within. By reason of the exceeding grace and of the light that is in them, men consider themselves free and perfect; but inexperience deceives them. They are under the influence of grace, but I have never yet seen a man that is free. I myself at times have in part come to that measure,

---

[1] Christensen, p. 80.
[2] Ted Campbell in Christensen, p. 81, note 22.
[3] Frank Baker, "John Wesley, Biblical Commentator," *Bulletin of the John Rylands Library* 71 (1989):111 f.

and I have learned to know that it does not constitute a perfect man.[1]

The "extracted" version of this homily, published by Wesley in *A Christian Library*, bears little resemblance to the independent translation above, and does not contain this particular passage at all, *as such*.[2] "Wesley, in appropriating the idea of theosis and constructing his doctrine of Christian perfection, found that the Church Fathers required editing."[3]

The logical conclusion of these factors is that Wesley effectively obscured, perhaps to himself as well, elements of Neoplatonic Mysticism that contributed to his doctrines of Prevenient Grace and Perfection, in some cases by failing to recognize them for what they were, and in other cases by carefully editing out overt references to the most objectionable concepts. This consequence has unfortunately served, due to Wesley's abiding popularity and influence, to introduce and establish erroneous views of Sanctification and related issues within a large segment of Christianity, including, *via* the Holiness Movement, some Perfectionist and Legalistic strains of Pentecostalism.

Even beyond this conclusion, problems associated with Wesley's exegesis must still be addressed, for which purpose three brief examples will suffice. Wesley uses the term, "the energy of love," to describe the "divine initiative" of God's Prevenient Grace, the "divine-human participation" by which man may attain Perfection.[4] Wesley engages Galatians 5:6, in particular, as a prooftext for this "energy" terminology. However, any first-year Greek student knows that while *energein* is indeed the etymological source for the English word, "energy," the Greek word literally means "work." Therefore, Theodore Runyon is mistaken in supposing Wesley's rendition to be "a literal translation" of the text,[5] which actually reads, "faith working through love." Contextually, righteousness rather comes by the instru-

---

[1] Pseudo-Macarius *Homily* 8:5, in A. J. Mason, *Fifty Spiritual Homilies of St. Macarius the Egyptian*, Translations of Christian Literature, Series I, gen. ed. W. J. Sparrow-Simpson and W. K. Lowther Clarke (London: SPCK, 1921), pp. 67 f.

[2] See *A Christian Library*, Wesley Center Online (http://wesley.nnu.edu/john-wesley/a-christian-library/a-christian-library-volume-1/volume-1-the-homilies-of-macarius/, accessed April 3, 2014).

[3] Christensen, p. 88.

[4] McCormick, p. 54.

[5] Runyon, p. 15.

mentality of faith (Gal 2:16, 3:6, 5:5, *et al.*), *because of* love; hence it is faith, not love, that does the work (and arguably faith is *cognitive* and *volitional*; not *affective*, as in the case of many definitions of love). Wesley's appropriation of the phrase, "energy of love," as well as the concept, can be traced back, again, to Chrysostom.[1]

Second, being challenged regarding the statement by James (3:2) that "we all stumble in many things," Wesley claims that "we" is just a "figure of speech," that James "could not possibly include himself," but rather refers "Not [to] apostles, nor true believers," but to others who will "receive the greater condemnation."[2] These claims are devoid of textual justification; rather, are obvious rationalizations and impositions on the text due to preconceptions ("analogy of faith," doctrinal construct) that are clearly contradicted by the passage.

Third, in prooftexting from John's first epistle, by which he argues that a person who has achieved Perfection *cannot* sin (or *does not* sin),[3] Wesley falls prey to errors common to "armchair" interpreters of that book, in particular: failing to account for the idiosyncrasies and alleged Hebraisms (too complex to detail here) inherent to it, but certainly including John's propensity for black-and-white dualisms and pointed use of the perfect participle. Most interpreters agree that John is describing those who make a regular practice of sin, or whose activities are by virtue of their unregenerated nature always characterized by sin, in contrast to the Regenerated. Worse, Wesley makes in this same context a claim upon Kingdom promises (Zech 12:8), saying, "The kingdom of heaven is now set up on earth." Thus he reveals a fundamental lack of understanding of eschatology, since the "fullness of the Kingdom" (including not only future glory but Perfection) will not come about till the Eschaton, the End. Elsewhere, among other examples, Wesley likewise fails to interpret Psalm 103:8, on the ultimate redemption of Israel, and 1 John 3:8, regarding Christ's complete work in overcoming sin and death, eschatologically.[4]

---

[1] McCormick, p. 102, note 153; McCormick, quoted in Troy W. Martin, "John Wesley's Exegetical Orientation: East Or West?" *Wesleyan Theological Journal* 26 (1991):136, note 114; see also Runyon, p. 15, note 30.
[2] Wesley, *A Plain Account*, p. 21.
[3] See *Ibid.*, p. 19 f.
[4] *Ibid.*, p. 41.

In fact, a studied perusal of Wesley's signature work, *A Plain Account on* Christian Perfection, on the whole reveals its proofs to amount to an exercise in unenlightened prooftexting—all done, one hopes, in ingenuous simplicity, by reason of the inadequate hermeneutical theory and tools of the day. Nevertheless, one cannot escape the inevitable conclusion that as a result of his long-term quest for personal, affective assurance, Wesley produced a compromise, "designer" religion that, however it might have shaded his exegesis, served his purposes more than it offended his strict British sensibilities.

Immanuel Kant (1724–1804)

Kant expressed Platonic ideas when he distinguished, in his *Inaugural Dissertation*, an intelligible, paradigmatic world from the sensible material world, a view he never relinquished in spite of later criticisms of Plato. He also appeared to strike a Platonic note later when, inspired by the empirical scientific "revolution" of Copernicus, he suggested that one's own metaphysical perception of reality might be judged as valid as that discovered by scientific observation.[1]

Karl Barth (1886–1968)

Early in his career, Barth was open in his admiration for certain historic figures, such as Mozart, Goethe, Schiller, Nietzsche, Kierkegaard, and in particular Russian novelist Fyodor Dostoevsky and the philosophers Socrates, Plato, and Kant. Dostoevsky was steeped in the beliefs and superstitions of the Eastern Orthodox Church, as well as widely read in philosophers such as Hegel and Kant.

Partly due to the influence of his philosopher brother, Heinrich, Barth placed Socrates and Plato on a level with Abraham and the Prophets in terms of inspired moral insight. He featured them alongside Biblical figures in his "*Lebensbilder aus der Geschichte der christlichen Religion*" lessons to the young girls of the congregation. Plato and Socrates, according to Barth, shared the ideals of the Prophets. Since "Jesus is, for us, not lesser but greater when we recognize him *everywhere*," these great pre-Christians act as "lights" and "mirrors" to reflect Christ to us. Kant further represented to Barth a "unique resur-

---

[1] "Immanuel Kant" in *SEP* at http://plato.stanford.edu/entries/kant/.

rection" of Platonic thinking, and therefore shares the limelight. Barth maintained these views at least through the authorship of his two Romans commentaries and his First Corinthians 15 commentary, *The Resurrection of the Dead*. He wrote, "It does not matter whether what they have and guard is Moses or John the Baptist, Plato or Socialism, or even the simple, daily activity of an inherent moral reason: it is calling, promise, the potential for a parable in this having and guarding, the offer and the open door of the deepest knowledge."[1]

In later years, Barth became more reticent about his enthusiasm for Socrates and Plato, admitting that his earlier works had a "remarkable crust of Kantian and Platonic ideas." "But look," he excused, "at that time I was strongly influenced—always influenced—by platonic philosophy. And like in the *Römerbrief* so also in this book on resurrection there are traces of Plato. And I stopped being a Platonist later on." So "then I was under the influence, well, from Plato, from Kant, from Dostojewski, from Kierkegaard and so on."[2]

Barth did not seem to be of a mystic bent, did not like using philosophical terms, and was critical of the intrusion of Metaphysics into theology in his day, yet does appear to have picked up a measure of Platonic, even Neoplatonic thinking. He echoed Plato's yearning for the Good and the Beautiful, fundamental motivations in Plato's search for transcendence. As in Plotinus' quest for the Fatherland, the Creation has forgotten God and longs to *return to the source*. As Kenneth Oakes summarizes, "Jesus Christ is the turning point of time and history, the *Tatsache*, the actuality, not as a philosopher or as a moral teacher, but because he is that which both Plato and the Old Testament prophets posited as the ideal: a man living in time and yet also living in eternity."[3] Judging as well from the way his contemporary, Ludwig Wittgenstein, used the term *Tatsache*, "fact," in his *Tractatus Logico-Philosophicus* (1922), it appears that Barth is thinking in terms of Christ as *Logos*, philosophically speaking, and ultimately as Platonic *form*; while Wittgenstein in parallel thinks in terms of a world created

---

[1] Kenneth Oakes, *Karl Barth on Theology and Philosophy* (Oxford University Press, 2012), pp. 32 f., 45, 64 f., 76, 97, 106, 239, 247; Gregg Strawbridge, "Karl Barth's Rejection of Natural Theology: Or an Exegesis of Romans 1:19-20," A Paper Presented to the Evangelical Theological Society, San Francisco, 1997), posted at http://www.wordmp3.com/files/gs/barth.htm.

[2] Oakes, pp. 76 note, 239.

[3] *Ibid.*, pp. 33, 45, 76.

of "facts" made up of "objects," which in turn build "pictures" of thought. "The picture," says his *Tractatus* 2.12, "is a model of reality"—or as one could well surmise, a *form*.[1]

Karl Rahner (1904–1984)

A Jesuit priest, Karl Rahner studied Kant and Joseph Maréchal, a transcendental Thomist, extensively, and during his doctoral studies became an especial devotee of existentialist Martin Heidegger, whose lectures he attended faithfully. One of Heidegger's peeves was Platonism in church tradition, in the sense of a transcendent spiritual world over the material. Rahner adopted this bias, and included Heidegger's as well as Maréchal's views in his doctoral dissertation, which was subsequently rejected. Nevertheless, he published the work in 1939 as *Geist in Welt*, a radical reinterpretation of Thomas Aquinas, which gained Rahner a popular following.[2]

Rahner was labeled as heterodox, if not heretical, and was placed under publishing sanctions by Pope Pius XII; but was soon favored by "progressive" Pope John XXIII with an appointment as advisor to the pivotal Vatican II Councils, where he emerged as a popular "star." "Rahner's influence was enormous," writes a critic. "He satisfied a modern world, and modern churchmen, whose ears were itching for doctrinal compromises under the pretext of 'enlightenment.'" During the Council, Rahner worked alongside another Progressive, Joseph Ratzinger, the future Pope Benedict XVI. It was revealed in 1994 that during the several years of Vatican II, Rahner wrote 758 letters to his longtime, ostensibly "Platonic" love interest, writer Luise Rinser. A double divorcee with two sons, Rinser professed Catholicism while delving into Buddhism, was a pro-abortion and anti-celibacy activist,

---

[1] Luigi Perissinotto, "'The Socratic Method!'": Wittgenstein and Plato," *Wittgenstein and Plato: Connections, Comparisons and Contrasts*, eds. Luigi Perissinotto and Begoña Ramón Cámara, (Houndmills, Hampshire, UK: Palgrave Macmillan, 2013), sec. 3; Robert B. Pippin, "Negation and Not-Being in Wittgenstein's Tractatus and Plato's Sophist," *Kant-Studien* 70 (1-4) (1979), p. 180; "Ludwig Wittgenstein" in *SEP* at http://plato.stanford.edu/entries/wittgenstein/.
[2] Thomas Sheehan, "The Dream of Karl Rahner," *The New York Review of Books* 29/1 (February 4, 1982) at http://www.nybooks.com/articles/archives/1982/feb/04/-the-dream-of-karl-rahner/; "Karl Rahner" in *Wikipedia* at http://en.wikipedia.org/-wiki/Karl_Rahner.

ran for German president with the Green Party, and lent her support to dictator Kim Il Sung of North Korea.[1]

Espousing views called the New Theology, Rahner and other advocates pressed to reform or redefine many Catholic dogmas. Earlier, Father David Greenstock had warned, "The main contention of the partisans of this new movement is that theology, to remain alive, must move with the times. At the same time, they are very careful to repeat all the fundamental propositions of traditional theology, almost as if there was no intention of any attack against it. This is very true of such writers as Fathers [Henri] de Lubac, [Jean] Daniélou, Rahner .... All of whom are undoubtedly at the very center of this movement."[2] Rahner's proposed doctrine of Transfinalization, intended to replace Transubstantiation, was condemned by Pope Paul VI in 1965.[3]

While outspoken against Platonic dualism (soul/body), Rahner's theology includes many Platonic as well as Neoplatonic and other Pagan elements. He believed in a unity of the soul with the body (Aristotle), and no "afterlife" as described in Christian revelation, but a "self-realization which embodies the result of what a man has made of himself during life,"[4] and only comes at death. So "if one maintains that man is immortal as a whole and not just as a spirit, then it follows for Rahner that in death one does not leave the material world but enters more deeply into it and becomes what he calls 'all-cosmic,' somehow present to and in communication with all material reality,"[5] i.e., a form of Pantheism. To Rahner, God's grace is built into nature, as is the soul itself, "Thus all persons are 'Christian'—that is, caught up in God's universal saving grace—by the very fact that they exist, regardless of whether they are baptized,"[6] which of course is Inclusivism or Universalism. God loves everyone and wants everyone to be saved, and can apply his Atonement as he wishes, apart from belief in Jesus.[7]

---

[1] John Vennari, "Karl Rahner's Girlfriend," *Catholic Family News* (May 2004), now reposted at http://www.freerepublic.com/focus/religion/1126324/posts.

[2] "Thomism and the New Theology," *The Thomist* 13 (1950), quoted in *Ibid.*

[3] "Karl Rahner" in *Wikipedia*; "Transfinalization" at CatholicCulture.org.

[4] Rahner, quoted in Sheehan.

[5] Sheehan.

[6] *Ibid.*

[7] Rahner referred to in "Religious Pluralism" in *SEP* at http://plato.stanford.edu/-entries/religious-pluralism/.

A concept of such "anonymous Christianity" (Rahner's term) "obviously changes the idea of missionary evangelization from 'telling the natives what they don't yet know' to 'showing them what they already are.'"[1] One recalls that "self-realization" was a necessary step in metaphysical *ascent*, going back at least as far as Plotinus; as to Plato the doctrine of the fallen entity drawn back to its source.   Liberation theologian Gustavo Gutiérrez also speaks in terms of "anonymous" Christians, in essence calling the masses of poor the Church, and therefore the temple of God and a "sacrament of universal salvation" (see Chapter 2 of this series). "We and the world are sacraments of God," writes Mark Fischer, and we "make the divine reality actual in our words and deeds."[2] To Fischer and other Rahnerians, the "Sacramental Principle" is that the material world *is* the spiritual world, such that human expression is an expression of God.[3] In essence, humans are thus the *effects* of God's *cause* in Christ, the *shadows* of his *form*, working in *theurgic*, Proclian, Dionysian *sympathy* toward the *source*, God.

"God established a world, not in a one-time act of creation, but in a constant process of divine causality [Proclian terminology], that is, in a relationship that is being 'continuously constituted' by God."[4] Christ came "in the flesh" as *Logos* only insofar as one is referring to "soul"; which Incarnation constitutes in itself "an act of creation."[5] Likewise, the Resurrection was not an "historical event" but a divine expression or concretization of God's identification with humanity.[6] Thus God "creates the human reality *by the very fact* that he assumes it as his own."[7] Rahner's redefinition of the Trinity, in Thomas Sheehan's opinion, "rehabilitates" it "by relating it to man's self-transcendence." As Sheehan summarizes, "Man knows the Father when he knows God as infinitely distant, he knows the Son when he knows God as absolutely close, and he knows the Holy Spirit when he knows God as penetrating existence and history," which statement is, by the way, a

---

[1] Sheehan.

[2] Mark F. Fischer, "Karl Rahner and the Immortality of the Soul," *The Saint Anselm Journal* 6.1 (Fall 2008), p. 1.

[3] *Ibid.*

[4] *Ibid.*, p. 8.

[5] *Ibid.*, pp. 10 ff.

[6] Sheehan.

[7] Rahner, italics his, quoted in Fischer, p. 10.

more or less exact reflection of the Platonic Trinity of "the One" (who lives in thick darkness), the Spirit, and the Soul (in that order).

Rahner's version of transcendence presumes the preexistence of souls (a Platonic concept) by presupposing that all humans have a "latent experience of God."[1] Integral with Rahner's theory of transcendence is the concept of "affective connaturality," a concept which Aquinas rationalized from Dionysius and Aristotle.[2] The term describes "intellect" not based on reason, nor from feelings or emotion, but intuitive and affective, by volition. Aquinas saw a "difference between the knowledge of divine reality acquired by theology and the knowledge of divine reality acquired by mystical experience,"[3] the latter of which in fact implies the Plotinian model of acquisition of divine knowledge through contemplative prayer, as discussed earlier.

Andrew Tallon defines that alternate kind of knowledge, or one might rather say *innate formative virtue*, as "the normal ... way the good person, the saint (... in the 'state of grace'), exists and acts as an embodied spirit, more highly actualized by virtues (some of them gifts of the Spirit), affectable and affected by God and then responding,"[4] which one presumes refers to the phenomenon of "spiritual forma-tion." Tallon further defines "affective connaturality" as "the essential 'mechanism' of ... intersubjectivity," the latter term having to do with the interrelating of two minds,[5] apparently expressing the theoretical *superimposition* of God's mind upon the human mind taught by Aqui-nas. Elsewhere, Tallon posits the instrumentality of "the life of the [small-'s'] spirit" through "prayer and action in reciprocal causation,"[6] which is perhaps comparable to a cause-and-effect *theurgy* of *sympa-thy* and *receptivity*.

There are two kinds of prayer, that which is direct and vocative (pre-sumably rational and cognitive), and that imaginatively called "dis-cernment of spirits ... consciously and responsibly bringing the rest of

---

[1] "Karl Rahner" in *Wikipedia*; see also Fischer, p. 11.
[2] See Jacques Maritain, *The Range of Reason*, ch. 3, online at http://www3.nd.edu/-Departments/Maritain/etext/range03.htm.
[3] *Ibid.*
[4] Andrew Tallon, "The Heart in Rahner's Philosophy of Mysticism," *Theological Studies* 53 (1992), p. 711.
[5] *Ibid.*, p. 709.
[6] *Ibid.*, p. 708.

life into free relation to the God addressed by prayer. Love of God and love of neighbor are traditional ways of saying the same thing.... The most perfect ethical action comes from discernment based on mystical attunement. The continuum of the ethical and mystical is again confirmed when the mystical as prayer becomes practical by flowing 'backward' as discernment."[1] Further, "The human soul, when more perfectly actualized by good habits (and, we hope, graced by the virtues that are gifts of the Spirit), approximates asymptotically the intuitive knowing and spontaneous love of the angels."[2]

The word *asymptotic* is a geometry term Tallon chooses, one gathers, to express approximation in the sense of replication that is nearly but not exactly perfect—suggesting "image" or "shadow" as compared to *reality* or *form*; and the realm of the angels is, of course, the higher realm of the Platonic *forms*. Moreover, Rahner (following Pierre Rousselot) "interprets Aquinas's hierarchy of spirit as meaning that the more perfectly actualized human soul (lowest in the hierarchy of spirits that includes angels and God) ... performs" on the highest level,[3] a concept lifted directly out of Pseudo-Dionysius, being that of the *hierarchs*, who alone may "contemplate, directly, the intelligible realm ... the realm visible and accessible to the angels," as described earlier.

So being Christian is reduced to arranging one's mental and behavioral patterns in a kind of semi-cognitive *Feng Shui*, in order to be attuned to more effectively channel the thinking and activities of the Spirit of God which one cohabits. The accomplished soul is then the one most imprinted with God's mind and conformed, through self-realization combined with a spiritual *osmosis*, in a process of *theopoiesis*, till achieving *apotheosis* or demigod status. This is a theology and methodology devoid of particular content and profoundly opposed to the New Testament revelation, wherein virtue is inculcated as it is instituted, through cognitive assent to the propositional truth of the Gospel, by receiving grace through obedience to the Gospel and Christ's commands, and trust in his provision, and by accepting the promised gift of the Holy Spirit: by whose continuing grace, in terms of enlightenment, empowerment, and encouragement, the believer can

---

[1] *Ibid.*, p. 708.
[2] *Ibid.*, p. 714.
[3] *Ibid.*, p. 713.

"perform" above mere human levels in order to overcome sin and "bear" righteous "fruit of the Spirit."

Pope Benedict XVI (b. 1927)

As mentioned earlier, Joseph Ratzinger worked with Karl Rahner at Vatican II. While conservatively Catholic in many ways, Ratzinger shares many theological perspectives with Rahner, has worked alongside Hans Küng and Edward Schillebeeckx, as well, and follows Neoplatonists Jean Daniélou and Hans Urs von Balthazar, and Metaphysicist René Guénon.

"Ratzinger is convinced that the dialogue between Judeo-Christian biblical faith and Hellenistic (neo-Platonic) philosophy has been providential."[1] The true God, as "the ground of all being," is the same the philosophers sought.[2] Indeed, Ratzinger holds that the world emanates from a greater reality and seeks to return to the Source,[3] a generally Platonic and specifically Proclian/Dionysian idea. To him, being "called by and to God" culminates in incorporation into the "God-initiated" or "God-permeated" world continuum ("*Einfügung in den durchgottete Kosmos*"), a world that is "sacramentally structured" such that it directs the creature back to the Creator,[4] again a Proclian/Dionysian concept.

In defending Sacramental Realism, Ratzinger deprecates the "idealist misjudgment of human nature" and the "naïve idea of man's spiritual autonomy" for which Immanuel Fichte is known, and by which Rudolf Bultmann concluded "that spirit cannot be nourished by matter." This "Idealistic heresy," according to Ratzinger, is relative to Marxist ideas and due to materialist thinking based on human effort—*homo faber*—"which thinks it knows again that man can only be spirit in the manner of bodilyness" and "want[s] to make man into a pure spirit before God." The sacraments, on the other hand, are vital as God's

---

[1] Boeve, p. 8.
[2] Nicholas J. Healy, "Natural Theology and the Christian Contribution to Metaphysics: On Thomas Joseph White's Wisdom in the Face of Modernity," *Nova et Vetera* 10, No. 2 (2012), p. 540.
[3] Boeve, p. 8.
[4] *Ibid.*

way of meeting man on a human level, using material means which embody "incarnation," "historicity," and the presence of Christ.[1]

Here Ratzinger falls back, unfortunately, upon a *theurgic* view of symbols and shadows which appeal to corresponding spiritual realities. Moreover, Ratzinger's dichotomy on human nature is a false one since, far from Fichte's totally man-centered view, the Biblical view is that man is a rational being capable of making choices of what to believe, whether to obey, and whether to "walk in the Spirit" daily, as opposed to "by the flesh, to fulfill its lusts." True, man is helpless to save himself, apart from grace; but the activation of grace is by rational choice in response to propositional truth, not dependence upon material sacraments or sacerdotal auspices. To Ratzinger, in contrast, the soul of man is not autonomous but part of a world-spirit destined to be restored as a body to God. His view relies more on "natural theology"[2] and historical Church theology than Scripture, which leads him to a view of Inclusivism that has spawned suspicions of Universalism, as did Rahner's.

The sacramental view, contends Ratzinger, is proven typologically, not rationally or empirically; by looking forward, not backward. He who clings to exegesis and the historical study of Scripture is "elitist," an "analyzer" who is "unspiritual" because he "imagines himself to be the initiate," presuming to "always know better" and "to be wholly spiritual."[3] "Historical reconstruction" fails to see "the unity of typological history."[4] This "narrowly conceived, purely salvation-historical view" fails to apprehend the "mystery." Yet the hidden wisdom is "simple," revealed to "fools," and "promises … entry into the innermost thinking of God." Mystery is effectual for "The one who lives and stays in the simple unity of the universal Church."[5] Meaning "is no longer the meaning of a biblical text" but of an "event, which reaches down to the center of creation and reaches up to the innermost

---

[1] Joseph Ratzinger, *Die sakramentale Begründung christlicher Existenz* (Freiburg im Breisgau, DE: Herder Verlag Herder, 2008), translator unknown, excerpted at http://www.novusordowatch.org/benedict/sbce-trans.htm; see also Healy, pp. 559 f.

[2] See Healey.

[3] Ratzinger, "On the Meaning of the Sacrament," trans. Kenneth Baker, in *FCS Quarterly* (Spring 2011), p. 30.

[4] *Ibid.*, p. 33.

[5] *Ibid.*, p. 30.

and definitive will of God."[1] One is reminded of the suggestions earlier by Fathers Keefe and Keleher to quit worrying and learn to trust
the Church.

Ratzinger does not initially ground his claim of *mystery* relative to
sacrament in the New Testament, in which the connection is conspicu-
ously absent. He first consults the Old Testament Wisdom books and
Apocrypha, then late rabbinical commentaries, then sacramental views
expressed by the Church Fathers (see Chapter 6 of this series), which
he afterward applies by virtue of the Catholic *analogy of faith* and with
reference to *typology* to reinterpret New Testament content by what he
deems a typological and sacramental "hermeneutic."[2] In Ratzinger's
hermeneutic, parabolic speech in Scripture which is literally unintelligible nevertheless better represents reality. Thus to "Rabbi Paul," the
mysteries of the Old Testament and the parables of the New "become
visible" in Christ, and "a word of creation."[3] More than that, "Jesus is
the meaning of all the words in the Scripture." Therefore, "not only
the words, but also the realities described by them are mysteries, em-
blematic references to Christ";[4] to the Sacramentalist, Christianity is a
mystery expressed in "symbols" which "reveal reality" and by which
one may "gain access to reality"[5]—the sum total of which suggests
theurgy.

All of Scripture, concludes Ratzinger, is a sacrament, both literal
words and "events."[6] His typological "understanding of the sacraments," as a creative hermeneutical *gnosis*, "presupposes the historical
continuity of God's activity and, as its concrete locus, the living community of the Church, which is the sacrament of sacraments,"[7] a view
of the church entirely amenable to the concerns of John A. T. Robinson and Gustavo Gutiérrez. Further, "The meaning of creation, which
appears in Jesus as the unveiling of the Scriptures, is unity in which
the fullness of God shines forth and illumines."[8] The sacramental un-

---

[1] *Ibid.*, p. 31.
[2] *Ibid.*, pp. 29 ff.
[3] *Ibid.*, p. 30.
[4] *Ibid.*, p. 31.
[5] *Ibid.*, p. 28.
[6] *Ibid.*, p. 31.
[7] *Ibid.*, p. 34.
[8] *Ibid.*, p. 31.

derstanding "purifies" and "refashions" creation continually[1] until "the Church, in which no longer Israel alone, but all mankind is drawn into the unity of love that leads to an indissoluble merger into one single existence."[2]

This "indissoluble merger" (*unlöslicher Verschmelzung*, "unfathomable fusion")[3] describes incorporation of souls *not* into an eschatological "kingdom-come," nor an exodus from darkness to light, from hell to heaven, as in the New Testament, but a *continuum* ("unity") of God's work upon the world, in all peoples, at all times and in both Testaments, amounting to a Plotinian *ascent* in knowledge of God— not however as individuals, but corporately as the Church. From the Old Testament to the New, one *ascends* from "the oppressive multiplicity of what is not yet transparent, to the liberating simplicity of what is Christian," then to rites which Ratzinger reckons to be open, transparent, and rational[4]—yet "mysterious" and symbolic?—until the day when God brings all things and all peoples, Catholics, Jews, and others, into him in unity and love, which echoes Robinson's conception of the *Parousia*.

Thus one observes Neoplatonism and Theurgy, along with the method called "analogy of faith," employed at will, eclectically, when convenient to theology and argumentation, and arguably so interwoven into the fabric of sacramental and mystical theology that its use, as well as its origins, may be utterly unconscious on the part of the practitioner.

---

[1] *Ibid.*, p. 32.

[2] *Ibid.*, p. 31.

[3] Séan Corkery, "Christological Hermeneutic: Sacrament and Scripture in the Work of Joseph Ratzinger," a paper presented to the 50th International Eucharistic Congress, Maynooth, Ireland, June 6, 2012, p. 4.

[4] Rat., "Meaning," p. 33.

Chapter 8. Pentecostalism *versus* Mysticism

Since first publishing the foregoing series of articles, the allegation that Pentecostalism constituted a form of Mysticism persisted. Therefore, the writer has deemed necessary some additional definition of Pentecostalism, as a practice and a theology, over and above the preceding definition of Neoplatonic Mysticism. The following represents summary conclusions, to date, based on available information, evidence, and personal experience, and likely comprises the initial installment in a long-term, ongoing study.

Mysticizing Pentecostals often claim that Pentecostal spirituality is a form of Mysticism, therefore mystical practice is no threat to and indeed compatible with New Testament-based Pentecostalism.

As a third-generation Pentecostal and trained Bible interpreter, however, I maintain that Mysticism and its practice—*e.g.*, *Contemplative Prayer* and *introspection* with the aim of Transcendence and "spiritual formation"—represent a foreign and alternate spirituality to that intended and prescribed by the New Testament. Heretofore, I based this contention largely on the absence of New Testament support for mystical practice, especially in terms of clear didactic statements (*i.e.*, New Testament believers are neither commanded nor taught to pray contemplatively, to chant *mantras* or empty the mind of thought); and conversely, on important commands and practices in the New Testament that are often discounted or ignored by Mystics.

A primary example of the New Testament practices often lacking among Mystics is the apostolic emphasis on becoming baptized in the Spirit, to be followed by manifestations of charismatic gifts. Many Mystics apparently deem Spirit Baptism, as described in the New Testament, unnecessary, irrelevant, and even redundant to their mystical practice and emphasis. Some Mystics claim to have transcended these elements of Pentecostal spirituality, identifying them with the "childish things" described by Paul in 1 Corinthians 13:11. Never mind the essential "enablements" that Jesus, in the "Paraclete passages" of John 14-16, promised that the Paraclete would provide, as well as Paul's admonitions to "be filled with the Spirit" and "edify" others through gifts. Mystics seem to leave little for the Holy Spirit to do: they together with God can do it all. Mystics purport to be able to touch God and be changed into Christ's image through methodologies and "spiritual disciplines" (see more below).

More recently, in response to debates with Mystics and Sacramentalists, and the occasion of a Contemplative Prayer guru being invited to speak at an event surrounding the 2013 General Council of the Assemblies of God, I embarked on further research from the opposite angle—that of Mysticism—beginning with its origins.

My research strongly suggests that the main stream of Mysticism throughout Church history has been the Neoplatonic type that appears to have originated, as such, with the philosopher Ammonius Saccas, passed along through his students. These include the Pagan philosopher Plotinus and the Christian theologian Origen of Alexandria. Building on the Platonic idea that the real world is that of the mind, from which the physical world has fallen, Neoplatonists imagined the possibility of ascending back to an ideal, divine state through contemplation of God, self-introspection, and other mental exercises. These ideas were passed along through the speculative theologies of such major figures as Gregory of Nyssa, Augustine, Thomas Aquinas, Meister Eckhart, Teresa of Avila, and even John Wesley.

Having become familiarized with Mysticism in addition to Pentecostal spirituality, I can now begin to describe differences between the two. Because of many variations in mystic practice and detail, it will be necessary to generalize, to which exception will no doubt be raised by obverse critics. However, exceptions hardly disprove the rule. Things which seldom occur represent exceptions, things which happen occasionally represent episodes, things which happen frequently represent trends, whereas things that are largely and regularly true make up the rule, regarding which one may generalize without justifiable contradiction.

To begin, the Pentecostal experience is not an *ascent* of a human being to God or attainment of divinity, but a *descent* in which God deigns to deposit, by measure, part of his nature or person, such that his Spirit cohabits flesh. As such, Spirit Baptism represents a parallel or reflection, if not technically a replication, of the very Incarnation of

Christ. Once received, the Holy Spirit is immanent, and need not be ascended-up-to.

Mystics, going back at least to Plotinus, have suggested that the "spiritual formation" engendered through Contemplative Prayer can enable God to be superimposed over the intellect or personality of the Mystic. That view, however, is contrary to New Testament examples and to Paul's assertion that "the spirit of the prophet is subject to the prophet" (1 Cor 14:32). It remains that a Spirit-filled believer may "quench" as well as "grieve" the Spirit (1 Th 5:19, Eph 4:30) through, one surmises, willful sin, resistance, or neglect. A long-held tenet among Pentecostals has been that "the Holy Spirit is a gentleman" who will not force himself upon the individual believer or overrule his or her free will. According to Paul the Apostle, the "mental exercise" involved, if so there be, is the believer's daily as well as immediate moral choice to "reckon" himself "dead to sin" and to "walk by the Spirit," not "by the flesh, to fulfill its lusts" (Rom 6:11, 7:5 f., 8:1 ff., 13:14; 2 Cor 1:17, 10:2; Gal 3:3, 5:16, 25). At all times, in the New Testament view, the believer remains subject to human nature, and can never with carefree permanence rise above it in this life. Watchfulness for one's soul is always enjoined, such that Paul himself regretted that he could never count himself to have "attained," nor discount the possibility of being in the end "cast away" (Php 3:11 ff., 1 Cor 9:27).

In Mysticism, one's human nature can ostensibly be transformed through "spiritual disciplines" and methodologies (one might say "methodism"), which include fasting and other ascetic practices, "purificatory virtues" (Plotinus), self-abnegation, contemplation, affirmation and negation, self-introspection, emptying oneself, guided visualization, chanting *mantras*, etc. (Such methodologies, utilized by Pagans, are known to produce altered states of consciousness through self-hypnosis.) Some would add participation in Sacraments. To the Pentecostal, in contrast, the human mind is consciously "transformed" (Rom 12:1 ff.) through believing Biblical revelation, adherence to correct doctrine, and submission to the Holy Spirit.

The Mystic craves Transcendence over human nature and worrisome matters of this life, and constant or frequent assurance of God's favor, God's existence, and one's own salvation. He (or she) longs to rise above petty humanity, to be unfettered by exigencies and rules, to eschew doctrine, debate, and "contending for the faith." He is emotions-based, desires to experience constant warm feelings and inner joy, and tends to be preoccupied with personal spiritual and moral development. The Pentecostal does not expect Transcendence except to the extent that he can resist and overcome base desires, by volition, when they arise. He is not driven to seek constant assurance, but stands by faith in the face of contrary feelings and circumstances. (Where is faith if one receives constant assurance?) He is encouraged ("edified") and his faith strengthened by sound teaching, meditating on Scripture, and periodic occurrences of charismata within the church Body ("signs and wonders"), especially the exhortation and consolation produced through prophetic gifts. As Paul instructed in the face of anxieties, "Wherefore, comfort one another with these words" (1 Th 4:18).

Contemplative Prayer, to the Mystic, is a standard methodology facilitating *ascent* towards God. The Incarnation is viewed in terms of Christ showing people the path to God toward their own self-divinization. *Ascent* amounts to here-and-now restoration, in part or in full, from fallen human nature, toward an original or rightful divine nature. To the Pentecostal, on the other hand, Spirit Baptism represents reception by grace of divine power coming to reside, through faith, within fallen humanity—by virtue of which God deigns to reclaim human nature through the partial impartation of himself to mere "earthen vessels," which are sanctified, not in their own right, but by his presence and influence. He comes to dwell not in deified flesh but in "all kinds of flesh"; not in response to an *ascent*, but by effecting a *descent*. "I will come to you," Jesus said, in the form of the Paraclete (Jn 14:16-18).

The Mystic desires God's immediacy, to realize divinization and Transcendence *now*. He rejects human nature and limitations, to seek *apotheosis*, *theosis*, *theopoiesis*, becoming God (pick one!). He seeks to put substance to faith: to experience, now, the object of Christian hope, to attain the object of faith before the culmination of all things. He is not content to wait or to "know in part" (with which the apostolic generation had to content themselves, *cf.* 1 Cor 13:9-12). Many Mystics develop an attitude of superiority by virtue of their passion for God's presence and for Transcendence, not unlike the Corinthian spiritualists who became "puffed up" in their enthusiasm for public charismatic displays.

Pentecostal spirituality is *eschatological*: "fullness" (culmination) comes at the *Eschaton*, the End. Man remains fully human, undivinized, mortal, until "changed" (1 Cor 15:51 f., Php 3:21). Our treasure is in heaven, our future inheritance. The deposit of the Holy Spirit, together with gifts, are the "earnest" of that inheritance (2 Cor 1:22, 5:5; Eph 1:11-14). Until the End, faith, not actualization, nor realization, remains the "substance" of the believer's hope, the assurance of things yet invisible (Rom 8:24, Heb 11:1).

Spirit Baptism is human nature eschatologically redeemed. It is incarnation, becoming God's instrument in spite of the flesh: "Christ in you, the hope of glory" (Col 1:27). Our hope (salvation, Eternal Life, divinization), as an object, is not yet available for our experience in this mortal life. At the "Last Trump" shall "mortal put on immortality" (1 Cor 15:3 f.), not before.

Mystics tend to dislike doctrine and dispute as something beneath their new apotheosized nature; but doctrine and debate, according to the New Testament pattern, are integral with declaring the Gospel before "the disputers of this Age" (1 Cor 1:20), along with preaching, rebuking, and exhorting (Titus 2:15, *et al.*).

To the Mystic, *ascent* obviates Spirit Baptism and gifts. Those who ascend enter into their own spiritual hierarchy. Those who reckon themselves on the path to *ascent* develop a "me and Jesus" attitude. They often gravitate toward Quietism, become monks and hermits. Their spiritual hierarchy tends to bypass church hierarchy and leadership, though they often seek out guru-type figures who can lead them into Ascension. Church, as an authority and teaching hierarchy, as a worshipping and self-ministering Body, and as a means of spiritual growth, tends to diminish in value in their eyes as they become "lone wolves" or "gurus" in their own right. They are too "transcended" to be subject to earthy rules, structures, and limitations.

The Pentecostal conceives a Church-as-Body-of-Christ model, with many parts variously functioning, all capable of individual, respective spiritual endowments, cooperating to form a whole. Thus they demonstrate why the "tongues of fire" lit upon each one individually at Pentecost (Acts 2:3). None are "higher" or "lower," none more or less ascended, only differing in gifts. All have the same Spirit (1 Cor 12:4 ff.). Individuals are gifted with immediacy, as the Spirit determines (1 Cor 12:11), requiring willing cooperation of the "prophet" but not ascent, purificatory rites, prior divinization or "spiritual formation." The motivated individual receives an influx of the Spirit, thus becoming temporarily a vessel "filled with the Spirit" (see "refillings" in Acts 4:8, 13:9). He is an instrument of the Divine ("a vessel unto honor, made holy, fit for the Master's use, and prepared unto every good work," 2 Tim 2:21), not divine himself.

Mystics rely heavily on a relative few passages of Scripture for support as well as devotional utility. Especial favorites are allegorical passages such as the *Song of Solomon* and parts of *Proverbs*. Such texts, comprised as they are of figurative literature, are ripe for abuse. In the minds of Mystics, the *Song*, for one, portrays a mystical pursuit of God, the soul wooing and being wooed, catching glimpses of God through Contemplative Prayer and ascent. Such applications of the Song go back at least to Origen.

Somewhat more compelling, in terms of a Biblical argument for Mysticism, are Moses' yearning to glimpse God (Ex 33), and Paul's vision of, or transportation to, the "Third Heaven" (2 Cor 12:1 ff.). Both narratives, however, actually tell against the possibility of mystical Transcendence, of approaching God, and of mere mortals becoming divinized. Such application of the Moses episode can be traced back to Philo, and was a frequent resort of Gregory of Nyssa. Much like today's Mystics, Moses yearned for a close encounter with God. Indeed, Moses is allowed to approach the vicinity of God's presence, but cannot be said to do so in a transcendent way (certainly not *via* Contemplative Prayer); rather, he comes, literally and physically, to the mountain bearing tablets to be written upon by the "finger" of God. God denies the feasibility of Moses seeing his "face" and surviving. He offers instead to allow Moses to see his "goodness"—the expression of his essential nature—and the after-effects of his glory or presence departing. Thus Moses can be said to experience God's influence but not at all God's real, full presence, nor Moses his own Transcendence. He sees God's effect, God's expression, but not God (much as any person, Romans 1, can see God in his Creation, only in greater measure). He is affected by the experience, but not ascended. The afterglow from God's presence which caused his face to shine was likewise an after-effect that was passing away, and represented neither a fundamental change in Moses' spiritual status nor his state of being, nor did God's glory become Moses' own lasting attribute or possession.

It might have been Moses' concern over the fading of this ascribed glory, which the people might have gathered to be a removal of God's blessing on his leadership, that caused him to cover his face after speaking to them.

In contrast, Paul's "visit to Heaven" was of a spiritual, revelatory character and not a physical approach to God. Yet to claim Paul's experience to have been accomplished through Contemplative Prayer would be sheer assumption, as would be the details of that experience, other than the fact of "hearing unspeakable words" and his subsequent receipt of a "thorn in the flesh." Paul's point in relating the episode is his realization and God-given reminder that it is not in any exalted experience, or seeming encounter with the presence of God, or "abundant" nature of divine revelations, or gifts of power, that he should glory, as if he were deserving, special, or accomplished, but in the power of the Cross and the grace that is "sufficient," in spite of the utter helplessness of the flesh (see also Gal 6:14).

In both these narratives, God's reply to seekers is that we can but reflect his glory. He alone is God, He gives his glory to no other. Though He may at times allow a glimpse, no man can attain any measure of godhood nor approach his throne. Try as we might, and yearn as we will, we remain mortal, subject to corruption, and cannot rise above it until eventually and finally Redeemed—indeed, a vital lesson every Mystic needs to learn.

Appendix

The Gnostic Christ

Gnosticism vs. Christianity

By the end of the second century, a religio-philosophical phenomenon on the fringes of Christianity had already been sharply defined by orthodox theologians and severely distanced from orthodox circles. This separation was performed expeditiously and effectively by such great orthodox leaders as Hippolytus, Tertullian, and most notably by Irenaeus in his *Against Heresies*.

This phenomenon is known today as Gnosticism. It was studied with interest in the twentieth century, especially since the discovery of a ruined Coptic library of Gnostic texts at Nag Hammadi in Egypt in 1947.

But why did the orthodox Church object so to this religious strain? And why the renewed excitement among modern religion scholars? The answer is the same on both counts: the thought of the Gnostics represents a variety of interpretation and application of the Christian message that differs from the orthodox view.

The most important point of departure from orthodox teaching is in the Gnostic redefinition of the meaning, purpose, and nature of Christ.

Is the Gnostic interpretation valid? Is it indeed Christian? Some Liberal scholars consider it equally valid with the Christian message. The Gnostics, however, appear to be affected by considerable religious and philosophical thought that lies outside the Judeo-Christian orthodox continuum. Perhaps the answer—or part of it—can be discovered by examining the sources of the Gnostic view of Christ, and the construct of Christ's nature and purpose they derive from those sources.

Definition of Terms

"Gnosticism" is a modern term[1] applied to a number of religious groups that placed an emphasis on esoteric knowledge (*gnōsis*) which is passed along, presumably, through the ages among those whom can be said to have "arrived," that is, achieved some higher spiritual plane.

---

[1] See Casey (*JTS* XXXVI [1938], 60), cited by R. McLaglan Wilson, "Gnostic Origins," *Vigiliae Christianae* 9 (1955):195, see also 193.

One can refer to things "gnostic" in the broad sense or in the narrow sense.[1] The broad sense is most appropriately rendered "gnostic," with a lower-case "g", in that it refers to the fact of an esoteric knowledge, or to certain traits or tendencies generally associated with known Gnostic religions. In this way, New Testament passages might be, and often are, alleged to be "gnosticizing." Two examples are: (1) references to the gospel as "saving knowledge"; and (2) the use of terminology—notably by Paul—such as "knowledge," "all things" (*tá pánta, e.g.,* "the All"), "fullness" (*plērōma*), *etc.*, which were at times employed as Gnostic technical terms.

Conversely, it is appropriate to refer to traits, practices, elements, *etc.*, as "Gnostic," with a capital "G", when applied to what is by definition a specifically Gnostic religion. A working definition of Gnostic religion will follow in the next section.

Two more terms must be contrasted: "pre-Gnostic" and "proto-Gnostic." According to the definition adopted at the Messina congress on Gnostic origins in 1966, "pre-Gnostic" refers to elements that existed before Christianity and were later incorporated into Gnostic religions. A "proto-Gnostic" element, on the other hand, is one that belongs specifically to the early stages of the formation of a Gnostic religion.[2]

Finally, one last term may now be defined, that is, "pre-Christian Gnosticism." In the twentieth century, there was considerable debate whether (1) Gnosticism as a religion preceded and developed in parallel or even in tandem with Christianity; or (2) it developed more or less directly from Christianity and existed as a Christian heresy.

The view of Gnosticism as a Christian heresy prevailed until at least 1909, when Robert Law proposed Hellenistic-Oriental Gnostic origins.[3] Later, Rudolf Bultmann became a major figure in a school of thought (following Richard Reitzenstein's hypothesis) that saw Gnosticism as both preceding and affecting Christianity,[4] and Gnos-

---

[1] See Edwin M. Yamauchi, *Pre-Christian Gnosticism*, 2d ed. (Grand Rapids: Baker Book House, 1983), 16 f.

[2] *Ibid.*, 18.

[3] Wilson, "Gnostic Origins," 194.

[4] See Edwin M. Yamauchi, "Jewish Gnosticism?" in *Studies in Gnosticism and Hellenistic Religions*, ed. R. van den Broek and M. J. Vermaseren (Leiden: E. J. Brill, 1981), 469-477.

ticism as equally valid from *religionsgeschicte* point-of-view. To call Gnosticism "pre-Christian" implies a view similar to Bultmann's.

In recent years, the pendulum has largely swung back to a more medial position. Bultmann's proposed Iranian origin of Gnosticism is today almost universally rejected.[1] Many scholars recognize pre-Christian elements having been incorporated into Gnosticism, but are critical of theories of a pre-Christian Gnostic religion such as that Bultmann constructed from post-Christian sources.

Delineation of Gnostic Religion

Because of the extensive variety of Gnostic and gnosticizing groups, it is necessary to provide a basic definition of Gnostic religion. In a 1967 article, T. P. van Baaren suggested in sixteen points the characteristics of Gnostic religion.[2] His points, however, are complex and sometimes overlap, and in some cases apply specific characteristics too broadly.[3] About the same time, H. Goedicke listed just four points,[4] which yet do not seem sufficiently in-depth. A more practical delineation of Gnostic religion is as follows:

1. A transcendent and impersonal God rules the heavens.
2. The material world is evil (i.e., *cosmological dualism*).
3. Man has fallen from a pure pneumatic (*i.e., spiritual*) state into the evil material realm.
4. God and the material realm are separated by a spiritual realm (the *plērōma*), filled with intermediate beings (*aeons*, "emanations," or "hypostases").
5. The material world is ruled by an evil *archōn* or *archōns* ("rulers") or Demiurge.
6. God at times sends redeemers to man to reveal a saving *gnōsis*.

---

[1] See Wilson, "Gnostic Origins, " 194, 207; Gilles Quispel, "Gnosticism from Its Origins to the Middle Ages," in *The Encyclopedia of Religion*, vol. 5, ed. Mircea Eliade (NY: Macmillan Publishing Co., 1987), 568; and G. Quispel, "Gnosticism and the New Testament,," *Vigiliae Christianae* 19 (1965):73.

[2] T. P. van Baaren, "Toward a Definition of Gnosticism," in U. Bianchi, ed., *Le Origini dello Gnosticismo* (1967), 178-180, quoted in Yamauchi, *Pre-Christian*, 14 f.

[3] Yamauchi, *Pre-Christian*, 14 f.

[4] *Ibid.*,15.

7. Through the esoteric *gnōsis*, man is able to save himself, regain his spiritual (pneumatic) nature, and in the end ascend to his place in the *plērōma*.
8. This salvation is available to a limited number of "elect" pneumatics.

This formulation should now provide a workable definition from which to continue this study.

Origins of the Gnostic Redeemer Figure

Most Gnostic redemption myths begin with the fall of Sophia ("Wisdom") to the earthly realm. This personified Wisdom figure might have been drawn directly from Old Testament and Apocryphal sources,[1] or from even more ancient Hebrew-Canaanite traditions.[2]

Sophia persuades the Demiurge, the evil creator of the material world, to give life to Adam,[3]—to the Naassene and Barbelo sects the "Primal Man."[4]   This Primal Man is identified by Bultmann as originating with the Iranian Primal Man/Redeemer myth.[5]   Bultmann has considered Mandaean texts to contain skeletal remnants of a more ancient Iranian prototype.[6] However, he commits a fundamental error in constructing a pre-Christian myth from post-Christian sources alone[7]—no extant Gnostic text can reasonably be dated earlier than the second century.[8]

Similarly, E. F. Scott postulates the origin of the Gnostic Primal Man in "some primitive myth, the meaning of which can now only be conjectured, and which possibly underlies the imagery of Daniel and

---

[1] See Yamauchi, "Jewish Gnosticism?" 489-90.

[2] See Quispel, "From Its Origins," 568.

[3] *Ibid.*, 570.

[4] E. F. Scott, "Gnosticism," in *Encyclopaedia of Religion and Ethics*, vol. 6, ed. James Hastings (NY: Charles Scribner's Sons, 1955), 236.

[5] Henry A. Green, "Gnosis and Gnosticism: A Study in Methodology," *Numen* 24 (August 1977):117.

[6] *Ibid.*, 116.

[7] *Ibid.*, 116 f., 123.

[8] See C. H. Dodd, *The Interpretation of the Fourth Gospel*, 98, paraphrased in Wilson, "Gnostic Origins," 205; Dodd is followed here against Wilson's own (unjustified) dating of Christian Gnostic origins to the mid-first century.

the Book of Enoch."[1] Here two hypotheses are yet to be established: (1) that Daniel and Enoch indeed utilized a more ancient myth; and (2) that the later Gnostic myth in turn descended from that of Daniel and Enoch.

Depending upon the specific variety of Gnosticism, either Sophia or the Primal Man exist in a fallen state[2] and require redemption. Until their redemption, the spiritual and material worlds co-exist in tension, in an imperfect and unacceptable state of admixture. At the prayer of Sophia (or "on his own initiative" in the Naassene material)[3] a Redeemer ("an Aeon of supreme rank—the Soter or Christus")[4] descends into the material world to rescue the fallen one. There are in fact numerous redeemer figures identified in gnostic and related literature.[5] From Judaism, directly or indirectly, come the figures of "the Great Seth" or "Illuminator";[6] Melchizedek/Seth;[7] the *descensus angelorum* (allegorized by Philo);[8] the "Light" or "Man" of Ezekiel;[9] the "Son of Man" of Daniel;[10] and certainly the figures of Jewish messianism and apocalyptic.[11] The "Teacher of Righteousness" of the Qumran sect (ostensibly Essene) has also been cited—but the Qumranians were essentially apocalyptists rather than Gnostics.

From Mesopotamia come many redeemer figures, notably Marduk and Mithra; and from Egypt, Osiris.[12]

Various Hellenistic sources are postulated. In Plato is found the *Ideal Man*, though the redemptive idea is absent.[1] It is alleged that in

---

[1] Scott, 236.

[2] *The Apocryphon of John* even "combines the Anthropos ["Man"] model and the Sophia model," Quispel, "From Its Origins," 570.

[3] Scott, 237.

[4] *Ibid.*

[5] See Yamauchi, *Pre-Christian*, 168.

[6] Gedaliahu A. G. Stroumsa, *Another Seed: Studies in Gnostic Mythology*, Nag Hammadi Studies, vol. 24, ed. Martin Krause, James M. Robinson, and Frederik Wisse (Leiden: E. J. Brill, 1984), 110.

[7] *Ibid.*, 111; see also Yamauchi, "Jewish Gnosticism?" 488.

[8] Wilson, "Gnostic Origins," 203.

[9] Quispel, "From Its Origins," 567.

[10] *Ibid.*

[11] G. van Groningen, *First Century Gnosticism: Its Origin and Motifs* (Leiden: E. J. Brill, 1967), 70-72.

[12] Scott, 237.

some Middle Platonic sources that "the translator of Ezekiel [1:26] in the Septuagint identifies the figure of divine Man with the Platonic idea."[2]   The Hermetic *Poimandres* (Hellenistic Jewish) posits an androgynous Phos/Zoe figure who descends and spawns mankind; Philo identifies the Divine Man or "Man of God" with the *Logos*.[3] However, only certain Gnostic systems coupled the *Logos* figure with the redeemer function. In other systems, *Logos* remained an entirely separate entity.[4]

The foregoing redeemer figures, with the exception of Philo and the Hermetic writings, do indeed represent pre-Christian elements alleged to later affect Gnosticism; yet none truly exhibits evidence of a Gnostic religion preceding Christianity, *i.e.*, "pre-Christian Gnosticism."

Redeemers more specific to Gnosticism are identified in Gnostic writings. "In the system of Simon Magus, Simon himself is the redeemer and appears in one form as Jesus."[5] *Pistis Sophia*, 369, refers to "Zorokothora-Meljisedek," according to F. C. Burkitt a corrupted coupling of the names Zoroaster and Melchizedek—but not in fact having anything to do with the historical characters. Only their names have been borrowed.[6]

John Dart describes two Gnostic redeemers which he considers to be in no way patterned after Jesus Christ. *Derdekeas*, in *The Paraphrase of Shem*, is touted as a "divine warrior" after the model of the Canaanite Ba'al or the Hebrew Yahweh.[7] In Dart's description, he seems to be nothing more than a fallen *aeon*, but does at times take on some function as Redeemer (or "Revealer").[8] The *Apocalypse of Adam* presents one called the Illuminator as a redeemer.[9] This figure does indeed (against Dart) appear to be based on a re-staging of the Incar-

---

[1] Cf. Quispel, "From Its Origins," 567 f.; see also Yamauchi, "Jewish Gnosticism?" 494; and Wilson, *The Gnostic Problem* (London: A. R. Mowbray and Co., 1958), 221, 226.
[2] Quispel, "From Its Origins," 568.
[3] *Ibid.*
[4] Yamauchi, "Jewish Gnosticism?" 480.
[5] Wilson, *Gnostic Problem*, 226.
[6] F. C. Burkitt, *Church and Gnosis* (Cambridge, Eng.: Cambridge University Press, 1932), 69.
[7] John Dart, *The Laughing Savior* (NY: Harper and Row, 1976), 97-101.
[8] *Ibid.*, 100 f.
[9] *Ibid.*, 101-103.

nation and Passion of Jesus. The Gnostic writings appear to adapt redeemer figures after either of two patterns: (1) ancient historical/ mythological/philosophical/legendary figures; or (2) the Christian presentation of Jesus Christ.

The Nature of Gnostic Redemption

Redemption in Gnosticism is not legal, ethical, or apocalyptic, as it appears variously in Judaism and Christianity. Gnosticism appears to be based on Persian *physical dualism* (*i.e.*, light versus darkness), but modified into a *cosmological dualism* of spiritual *versus* material.[1] The Gnostics hoped to transfer from this world to the spiritual realm, and ultimately into the *plērōma*, by the receipt of an esoteric *gnōsis*, *i.e.*, "spiritual enlightenment."[2] This *gnōsis* was brought, directly or indirectly, by a redeemer who acted as "revealer" to a select few of the "elect."

To the Gnostics, being awakened from their sleep and perceiving the knowledge, "gnosis," of their beginnings and destiny was "redeeming" for them. In other words, obtaining mystical knowledge of this kind was thought to be their salvation, and in that sense a revealer-figure was also a redeemer.[3]

The Gnostic Christ

Not all Gnostics cared to associate themselves with the figure of Jesus Christ. The Mandaeans are a sect that venerated John the Baptist, but rejected Jesus as a false prophet.[4]

Still, overall the Gnostics freely and readily adopted the Christ-image as their Redeemer, or the latest in a series of redeemers. "The grand characteristic of Christian Gnosticism is the identification of the mythical Redeemer with Christ, with whose history the pagan traditions are interwoven."[5] Jesus became to them a mystical figure: one

---

[1] Scott, 234.
[2] *Ibid.*
[3] Dart, 101.
[4] Yamauchi, "Jewish Gnosticism?" 469, 471.
[5] Scott, 237.

who, according to the Valentinians, clothed himself with the esoteric "Name of the Lord."[1]

Jesus did not, say the Gnostics, come to bear the sins of men, that whoever believes in his atoning death may gain eternal life. "The real purpose of Jesus, or rather to the Soter ['Savior'] who used Him as his instrument, was to communicate the hidden *gnōsis*."[2]

Most scholars consider the general Gnostic view of the Incarnation to be *docetic* (from Gk. *dokein*, "to seem"). This term, however, is usually applied to the early heretical position that Jesus was never actually present in the flesh, but only "seemed" to be human. He was, in this view, entirely spiritual and his human appearance an illusion. Thus Elaine Pagels is probably right in objecting to the docetic label.[3]

Instead, the Gnostic Christ had *two* natures: the pneumatic (spiritual) and the psychic (physiological). The Gnostics variously held that the Savior/Redeemer indwelt the earthly Jesus at birth (the Naassenes and the *Pistis Sophia*), at the age of twelve (the Justinians), or at his baptism by John (most sects).[4] The Valentinians believed that at his baptism Jesus received the "Name of the Lord."[5] The divine Savior departed from Jesus' body at the time of the trial before Pilate,[6] later while on the cross, or somewhere in-between. Basilides taught that Simon of Cyrene was transformed to look like Jesus and crucified in his place.[7] Such separation of Christ from the material world was evidently requisite in order to comply with Gnostic dualistic conceptions.

Thus the true (Gnostic) Christ escaped suffering and death.[8] Christ's death was not a redemptive act: it was merely due to an outburst of

---

[1] Quispel, "New Testament," 80, see also 82.
[2] Scott, 237.
[3] Elaine H. Pagels, "Gnostic and Orthodox views of Christ's Passion: Paradigms for the Christian's Response to Persecution?" in *The Rediscovery of Gnosticism*, vol. 1, ed. Bentley Layton, Studies in the History of Religions, vol. 41, ed. M. H. van Voss, E. J. Sharpe, and R. J. Z. Werblowsky (Leiden: E. J. Brill, 1980), 264.
[4] Scott, 237
[5] Quispel, "New Testament," 80.
[6] Pagels, 265.
[7] Dart, 108-109.
[8] See Irenaeus, *Against Heresies* 3.16.6; according to Pagels, however, the Valentinians affirmed the Passion of Christ, Pagels, 262-88; but the spiritual part of Christ still did not suffer, only the psychic (266).

wrath from the evil Demiurge.[1] The wholly spiritual Christ—according to Basilides, *The Second Treatise of the Great Seth*, and *The Apocalypse of Peter*—now laughed at the folly of his would-be executors.[2] They thought they could rid themselves of the divine Redeemer!

> He whom you see above the tree, glad and laughing, is the living Jesus. But the one into whose hands and feet they drive the nails is his fleshly part, which is the substitute . . . one made in his likeness.[3]

This "laughing" of Christ was possibly drawn from Psalm 2, concerning those who conspired "against the Lord and his Anointed," so that "He who sits in the heavens laughs; the Lord has them in derision."[4]

Summary

The Redeemer figure is one variously assembled from ancient myths and traditions. Then the figure of Jesus Christ was adapted and fitted into the Gnostic scheme as yet another redeemer. Just as Gnostic teachers appropriated Paul's terminology to their purposes, they also appropriated the figure of Christ.

The evidence adduced here does not suggest a Gnostic religion preceding Christianity—not as defined. There might have existed gnosticizing traits in some pre-Christian religious sects. There might be elements and terminology in primitive Christianity itself that can be called Gnostic. Yet Gnosticism as we know it from Nag Hammadi and related texts cannot be demonstrated before Christianity was well established.

Gnosticism is by nature syncretistic.[5] The Gnostic Jesus presented here is the natural byproduct of this syncretism, wherein elements pre-Christian and post-Christian; elements Egyptian, Iranian, Hellenistic, philosophical, *etc.*; and elements derived from specious exegesis and active imaginations have melded to produce a radically different Christ

---

[1] Scott, 237.

[2] Dart, 109.

[3] From *The Apocalypse of Peter*, quoted in Dart, 107.

[4] *Ibid.*

[5] See Dodd, *Fourth Gospel*, 97 f., quoted in Wilson, "Gnostic Origins," 197.

from that of orthodox Christianity—and one that is just as naturally labeled heretical by its opponents.

Select Index

Printed in Great Britain
by Amazon